All rights reserved by the Village of Oberammergau
Reproduction prohibited
Printed by: Fa. Buch- und Kunstdruckerei Hermann Weixler GmbH
Published by the Village of Oberammergau
Photos by Manfred Zirngibl
Translated by Translingua, Frankfurt a.M.
in consultation with Prof. G. O. Lang and M. B. Lang

The Oberammergau Play of the Suffering, Death and Resurrection of Our Lord Jesus Christ

Written in 1811/15 by Father Othmar Weis O.S.B.
on the basis of old texts

Revised in 1860/70 by Joseph Alois Daisenberger,
Ecclesiastical Counsellor

Further revised and published
by the Village of Oberammergau for 1990

Music composed in 1815/20 by Rochus Dedler
rearranged in 1950 by Professor Eugen Papst

For God loved the world so much that he gave his only Son, so that everyone who believes in him may not die but have eternal life. (Jn 3, 16)

Preface

The Oberammergau Passion Play has a long tradition. It dates back to 1633, when the village was afflicted by the plague which carried off many inhabitants in a short period of time. In peril of their lives, the people turned to Jesus Christ who suffered fear, torture and death on the Cross, but did not perish in doing so. Instead, he worked our salvation and gained life. Before the Cross the enlarged Village Council, the "Six" and the "Twelve", vowed to perform a Passion Play every ten years. Faced with the threat of death the village wanted to support its prayers with the vow which would be secured in history. God heard their prayers and the people of Oberammergau fulfilled their promise. Since then the Play has passed through every generation as a holy inheritance, as a celebration of remembrance of salvation from the peril of death and as an expression of gratitude. "In the Cross is salvation, in the Cross is life, in the Cross is hope" – this belief is intended to be kept alive in the village and the same message is addressed to the many spectators.

It was not by chance that the people of Oberammergau had the idea of the Passion Play. Passion plays were a much-loved and widespread form of religious folk play in old Bavaria and Swabia. Therefore it was not necessary to go far afield to seek the idea of the saving vow. It is also possible that the villagers of Oberammergau already had experience of a Passion Play and therefore knew that their promise would mean taking trouble and would be a challenge to the faith of the actors. This is still true today. The Passion Play is still an Oberammergau Passion. Fervent efforts, which also cause suffering, are made to achieve the correct, best possible form of presentation. So far as the content is concerned, even today acting in the Play entails a certain degree of pained perplexity and, in times of increasing secularisation, it demands that the players confront their own life style and inevitably raises the nagging question of identification.

The character of the Passion Play is also explained by its origin. Nowadays people would hardly dare to represent the Lord's suffering and death with such a carefree folk piety. The justification for today is in the true tradition which extends over centuries and has also overcome great difficulties. According to tradition, the Holy Play must be paid for, produced and acted only by inhabitants of Oberammergau because the Passion Play has been entrusted to them collectively as their inheritance. Therefore in spite of all the endeavours to give it proper artistic form and in spite of all the acting skill which has been developed and refined among the population as a result of the long tradition of the Play, it still remains a religious folk play. This is precisely what constitutes its attraction and expressive force.

Passion plays have their beginnings in liturgical endeavours to bring to believers the message of the Gospels concerning Jesus' suffering and death in the form of the folk devotions. Devotions at the stations of the Cross, devotions on the Mount of Olives, devotions on the five holy wounds and the seven words of Jesus on the Cross served and still serve the purpose of devout contemplation. These efforts also explain Passion plays which are, in essence, paraliturgical devotions on the Passion. This is a characteristic of the Oberammergau Play, which was performed for a long time in the graveyard, in the shadow of the church, and this made the connection between divine service in the church and the divine service of the Play particularly clear. This has not been altered by the fact that the Play has been moved into the Passion Theatre.

The Biblical basis of the Oberammergau Passion Play is a synopsis of all the Gospel texts, the harmony of the four Gospels. In the first place, this rules out the possibility of presenting the specific viewpoint of one Evangelist, which is complete in itself. However, it also aims to express and portray all the messages of salvation of the Gospels. This view of the Play excludes the updating of the image of Jesus, which would mean the Jesus of yesterday becoming the Jesus of today. It is in the nature of the Oberammergau Play to narrate visually the religious story of the suffering, death and resurrecting of Jesus in a way which is as faithful as possible to the Gospels. What the Play proclaims remains relevant for all time precisely for this reason.

In the course of time the structure of the Play has acquired an almost classical form. The events of the suffering of Jesus are shown in 14 acts and are constantly interrupted by the Prologue and the blending-in of scenes from the Old Testament. The speaker announces the scenes and interprets them in relation to our life. The chorus meditates upon the so-called tableaux vivants in song to show their relevance to the following act of the Passion. The fact that the Play is structured in this way promotes meditative assimilation of the material. The purpose is not only to keep the spectator informed, but also to let him think about what he sees. It is not enough simply to observe the Play, it should lead us to an encounter with this Jesus – our Saviour.

The present version of the text goes back to Father Othmar Weis of Ettal. When Passion plays degenerated during the Baroque and were prohibited in Bavaria, the text of the Oberammergau Play, which was faithful to the Bible, was scrutinised and found acceptable by the ecclesiastical and temporal authorities. The Passion Play was saved. The Oberammergau teacher Rochus Dedler composed congenial music to accompany the new text. Later Pastor Alois Daisenberger, the kind-hearted priest of Oberammergau who had an understanding of the arts, revised the text and rewrote the Prologue in classical metre. The structure of the text has remained substantially the same to this day, although almost every generation connected with the Play has worked on the text. In recent times extensive amendments have had to be made primarily on theological and ecumenical grounds, and these have not always been of benefit to the literary dramaturgical form. Overall, however, the Oberammergau Passion Play is characterised by the harmony of words, action and music and it is this combination of three elements which determines the total effect and the Play's importance as a universal art work in the category of religious folk plays.

To speak of the Oberammergau "Festival" is to mistake the special nature of the Passion Play. It is also inappropriate to describe it as "theatre". It is a mystery play because the fact is that the suffering of Jesus is not enacted for its own sake, but for the sake of the redemption which Jesus has gained by his suffering. By showing the victory of good over evil and of life over death, the Play is an encouragement to positive identification and helps people to dispel fears and to bear suffering because fears and suffering are sanctified by the Passion of Jesus and are in principle overcome by his resurrection. It is no doubt these aspects of deep belief which bring such large numbers of people to the Passion Play in Oberammergau. We therefore hope that the 1990 Play will be a witness of faith and a healing experience for the performers and for the many spectators.

Dr. Franz Dietl, Parish Priest

PRELUDE

Reconciliation and new life from the Cross of Christ

The life forfeited by Adam at the Tree of Paradise is won back by Christ on the Tree of the Cross

Bass solo: *Bow down in holy wonder,*
Race oppressed by God's curse!
Peace to you once more from Zion's grace!
His, the offended One's, anger does not last for ever,
Although it is still justified.
"I do not demand", says the Lord,
"The sinner's death; I will forgive him,
And he shall live!
My own Son's blood will reconcile him!"
Praise, adoration and tears of joy
To you, Eternal Lord!

Human kind is driven from Eden's grove,
By sin benighted and in dread of death.
Its way to the tree of life is, alas, barred.
The flaming sword looms in the angel's hand,

But from afar, from Calvary's heights,
A morning gleam shines through the night;
Soft breezes of peace blow throughout the world
From the branches of the Tree of the Cross.

Chorus: *God of Mercy! You give to death*
Your only Son, in order to redeem sinners
Who have blasphemously defied your commandments,
And to take the curse from them.

Prologue

Welcome to all whom here the tender love
Of the Saviour unites, mourning to follow Him
    On His journey of suffering
    To His final resting place.
All who from near and far have come today,
All feel themselves now joined in brotherhood,
    As disciples of the One
    Who suffered for all,
Who gave Himself for us
To the bitterest death.
    Let our eyes and hearts
    Be turned to Him united in gratitude.
Greetings also to you, brothers and sisters of the people
    Who brought forth the Redeemer.
Let no-one try to find the blame in others;
    Let each of us recognise
    His own guilt in these events.
God has made us all full of disobedience;
But to all He has brought mercy and salvation from the cross.
Pray with us as the hour comes
    When we pay the debt
    Of our sacred vow to the eternal God.

Bass/Tenor:
Eternal God! Listen to your children stammer!
Hear then their hearts and voices raised in thanks!
They who assemble at the great sacrifice
Worship you in holy veneration.

Follow now at the side of the Redeemer,
Until He struggles to the end
Of His rough and thorny path, and in fierce strife,
Bleeding to death, His sufferings end for us.

ACT 1

Christ's Entry into the Holy City of Jerusalem

1.

Jesus enters Jerusalem accompanied by the rejoicing of the people

Hail to You! Hail, Son of David!
The throne of the fathers belongs to You,
Who come in the name of the Highest,
bringing what is to profit us,
We glorify You! We glorify You!

Hosanna! May He who dwells in heaven
Send his grace to You!
Hosanna! May He who reigns above
Preserve You for us evermore!

Hail to You! Hail, Son of David!
The throne of the fathers belongs to You,
Who come in the name of the Highest,
bringing what is to profit us,
We glorify You! We glorify You!

Blessed be the realm and people of David,
Restored to their own again!
All you nations bless, praise and exalt the Son,
Like the father!

Hail to You! Hail, Son of David!
The throne of the fathers belongs to You,
Who come in the name of the Highest,
bringing what is to profit us,
We glorify You! We glorify You!

2.

Jesus drives the dealers from the temple court

Christ: What do I see here? Is this the house of God? Or is it a market place? Shall the strangers who come from foreign countries to worship God say their prayers in this crowd? And you, the priests and guardians of the sanctuary, see this abomination and tolerate it? Get out! I command you! Take what is yours and leave this holy place!

Several: Who is this?

People: The great prophet from Nazareth in Galilee!

Joshua: Why do you disturb these people?

Zadok: How can you forbid them what the High Council allows?

Ezekiel: Everything here is intended for sacrifice to God!

Boaz: Can we no longer offer sacrifices?

Christ: There is enough room for your business outside the temple! "My house", says the Lord, "shall be called a house of prayer for all people!" But you have made it a den of thieves! Clear it all out!

Archelaus: You can't do that!

Esron: My doves!

Kosam: My money!

Albion: My jars of oil overturned! Who will make good the loss?

Christ: Away with you! I want this profane place to be restored to the worship of my Father!

Zadok: On what authority are you doing this?

Several: By what miracles can you prove that you have power to do this?

Christ: You ask for miracles? I can give you one: destroy this temple here, and in three days I will rebuild it!

Ezekiel: It took forty-six years to build this temple, and you say you can rebuild it in three days?

Children: Hosanna to the Son of David!

People: Praise be to Him who comes in the name of the Lord!

Rabinth: Do you hear what they are saying?

Dariabas: Forbid them to do it!

Christ: Truly, I tell you: If they were to say nothing, the stones would cry out!

Children: Hosanna to the Son of David!

Ezekiel: Be quiet, you silly children!

Christ: Have you never read the text, "Thou has made children and babes at the breast speak aloud Thy praise"? What is hidden from the proud, is revealed to the little ones. And the scripture will be fulfilled: "The stone which the builders rejected has become the cornerstone." Any man who falls on that stone will be dashed to pieces, and if it falls on anyone he will be crushed by it. Come, my disciples, I have done what my Father commanded me to do. Now let us go inside the sanctuary and worship the Father there!

Children and people: Hosanna! Hosanna to the Son of David!

Nathaniel: Will you be quiet!

Children and people: Praise to the anointed One!

Oziel: You shall all be destroyed with Him!

Children and people: Praise be to the kingdom of David!

Children: Hosanna to the Son of David!

All: Hosanna! Hosanna!

3.

The priests try to win the people over

Nathaniel: Those who hold to the faith of our fathers stand by us.

Several: Why did you not seize him?

Other voices from the crowd: Should our High Priests have realised that Jesus is the Messiah?

Another group: He is a great prophet.

The others: He is the Messiah.

Several: Does the Messiah come from Galilee?

Archelaus: Scripture teaches that the Messiah comes from David's town of Bethlehem. But this Jesus is a native of Nazareth.

Nicodemus: Has he not healed sick people and made clean those who were possessed?

Joseph of Arimathea: Blind men can see and lame people can walk.

Several: He has only done good.

Ezekiel: Have you already been led astray? None of the High Priests believes that he is the Messiah.

Archelaus: He is a false teacher, an enemy of Moses and an enemy of the laws of our fathers.

Nathaniel: You people have been blinded! Do you want to follow this man with new ideas and leave Moses and the prophets? Children of Israel! Do you no longer wish to be God's chosen people?

Several: No!

People: Far be it from us to foresake Moses and his laws.

Nathaniel: But who is authorised to proclaim God's laws to you? Is it not the High Council of the people of Israel? Who will you listen to? Us, or this tempter who proclaims himself the founder of a new doctrine? (To Archelaus) Tell the high priests we are here.

Joshua: We will listen to them.

People: We will follow you.

Zadok: The God of our fathers will bless you for this.

Nathaniel: Friends, be calm. This man has too many followers. We shall go now to inform the High Council of what has happened today. Trust in us. Let us be your leaders.

Joshua: Praise be to our fathers!

The crowd: Praise be to the God of our fathers!

4.

Preparations for the arrest of Jesus

Nathaniel: High priests, fathers and elders! To our shame, with our own eyes we saw the triumphant entry of this Galilean, and how he marched through the gates and streets of holy Jerusalem. – You heard the hosanna cries of those deluded people. What remains before the complete overthrow of the whole government system and God's laws? One more step, and the holy law which God gave us through Moses will be overthrown. The doctrine of our fathers will be despised, the Sabbath profaned, the priests divested of their office, and the holy sacrifice at an end.

Ezekiel: Very true.

Several: Only too true.

Nicodemus: Why? Does the Galilean disregard the law?

Joseph of Arimathea: He has said that not a single word of the law should be taken away.

Caiaphas: Do not be deceived. When the Galilean came into the city, he had himself proclaimed by his disciples as the Son of David, the Messiah, and they will soon proclaim him the King of Israel. Then discord will arise among the people, there will be a revolt against the Romans and they will come with their armies and bring ruin to the land and people. Woe to the temple of the Lord and woe to us, the High Priests, if we allow his provocative behaviour and his arrogant speech in the temple to go unpunished. It is high time to avert the destruction of Israel. The Galilean has already gained too many followers. Friends and brothers, the responsibility is ours, the guardians of Zion. We must decide today what has to be done.

Several: Yes, today.

Caiaphas: Brothers, tell us plainly your opinion.

Archelaus: Honourable fathers, I believe we ourselves are partly to blame that this has gone so far. What was the good of our trying to embarrass him with questions, and proving to him his deviations from the doctrine of the fathers and his violation of the law? You can see that we have accomplished nothing. The people are turning their backs on us and the whole world is running after him. If there is to be peace in the country, what ought to have been done long ago must now be done without delay. We must get hold of him and throw him into prison – in a word, render him harmless.

Several: Yes, that is what we must do!

Nathaniel: That will make the proper impression on his followers and will cool their enthusiasm for him if he, who promises them freedom, is himself now in fetters.

Annas: Priests and teachers, at last there is a gleam of comfort and joy for my heart, as I observe your determination. Believe me, this Galilean's false teaching has often caused me great concern. But now I don't need to dispair any longer: The God of our fathers is alive and with us! Have courage, to be the deliverers of Israel! For this, undying renown will be yours.

Saras: The faith of our fathers must not perish.

Oziel: Israel must be saved!

Caiaphas: All honour to your unanimous determination! However, now you must help me with your advice so that we can lay our hands on the tempter as soon as possible.

Nathaniel: It would be dangerous to capture him now during the festival. Who would dare to take him prisoner – whether in the temple or in the street – because everywhere he is surrounded by a horde of delighted people? And at this moment, when thousands of people have reached the highest degree of enthusiasm?

Ezekiel: We must try to take him prisoner quietly, by a trick. We can certainly find out where he retires to for the evening. He can be arrested there and taken away without attracting attention.

Dathan: I know one of his followers. I hope to discover through him where he stays at night.

Caiaphas: If you can find one, make every promise in our name. But do not delay, so that we can achieve our object before the festival.

Annas: And keep quiet about it.

Dathan: I will.

Caiaphas: Now we shall see who will win, he and his followers – or we and our loyal supporters who obey the law.

Annas: May the Lord be with us.

All: Praise be to our God!

ACT II

Jesus' Parting from His Friends and His Mother Mary in Bethany

Prologue

He who with steady vision looks through the veil
Of the future, now sees the tempest approaching
Which gathers, threatening to burst upon His head.

Tarrying still in the midst of His own loved circle,
To these dear friends He speaks the word of parting,
A word which deeply wounds His loving Mother's soul.

See how full of sorrow Tobias' mother gazes at the son
    of her heart,
Departing, and in streaming tears pours out
The sorrow of her tender love.

Even so the Mother of the Son of God weeps
When she sees her beloved Son going with resolute steps
To wipe out with His love and death the sins of mankind.

1. Biblical Prefiguration

The young Tobias departs from his parents (Tob. 5, 17-23)

Tenor solo: *What a bitter grief, oh friends,*
Overcame the mother's heart,
As, guided by Raphael's hand,
Tobias at his father's word
Hastened to a foreign land.

Soprano/ *With lamenting and bemoaning*
Tenor: *She calls after her beloved son:*
"Come, do not delay,
O light and comfort of my soul!
Return soon in joy!

>   *O Tobias, dearest one,*
>   *Hasten back to me.*
>   *Dearest son, with you alone,*
>   *Can my heart gain content,*
>   *And have the greatest joy."*

Chorus: *Desolate now she laments,*
               No joy in her life,
               Until at some blissful moment
               Her beloved son is brought back
               To his mother's heart.

Prologue

See the bride in the Song of Solomon,
How she weeps for the missing bridegroom,
How she calls and seeks.
Allowing herself no rest until she finds him.

The pain in Mary's soul is more tranquil,
Although it pierces her heart like a sword,
The pain is softened
By her pious resignation, and trust in God.

2. Biblical Prefiguration

The loving bride laments the loss of her bridegroom (Song of Songs 3, 11 ff.; 6, 1 ff.)

Soprano solo: *Where has he gone, oh where,*
               Fairest of the sons of men?
               For him my eyes weep
               Hot tears of love.
               Come back! Return to me!
               See these tears flowing.
               Beloved, do you hesitate
               To clasp me to your heart?
               I seek for you everywhere,
               On all roads I look for you,
               And my heart hurries to meet you

>   With the first ray of the sun.
>   Beloved, ah, what do I feel?
>   How anxious is my heart!

Soprano solo/ *Dear companion, take comfort,*
Chorus: *Your friend will return.*
Wait, dear maid, soon he will return
And clasp you to his heart.
No cloud will again darken
The bliss of reunion.

The Passion

1.

Jesus announces His suffering and death to the disciples

Christ: My disciples, you know that in two days it is Passover. So let us take leave of our friends in Bethany and then go to Jerusalem, where shortly everything will be fulfilled which was written by the prophets concerning the Son of Man.

Philip: Is the day at last near when you will restore the kingdom of Israel?

Christ: None but the Father knows that day. But now the Son of Man will be handed over to the high priests and doctors of the law, who will condemn him and hand him over to the foreign power. He will be mocked, whipped and crucified, but on the third day He will rise again.

John: What does all this mean, Master?

Christ: The hour has come when the Son of Man shall be glorified. Truly, I tell you, a grain of wheat remains a solitary grain unless it falls into the ground and dies; but if it dies it bears a rich harvest. Now is the hour of judgement for this world; now shall the prince of this world be driven out. And I shall draw all men to myself, when I am lifted up from the earth.

Thaddeus: What does He mean by these words?

Simon: Why does He compare himself with a grain of wheat?

Andrew: Lord, you speak at one and the same time of humiliation and glorification, death and resurrection, shame and victory?

Christ: What is now as dark as the night to you, will soon be made as clear as day. I have told you all this so that you do not despair, whatever may happen. Have faith and hope. When the tribulation is past, then you will see and understand.

Thomas: Have we not heard from the prophets that the Messiah will remain for ever? How can you say, "The Son of Man must be raised up"? Who is this Son of Man? Anyone who, like you, wakens the dead, cannot die. Therefore, what can your enemies do to you?

Christ: Thomas, pray for the counsel of God, which you cannot fathom. For only a short time will the light be with you now. Walk in the light while you have the light, so that the darkness does not overtake you. Believe in the light, so that you become children of the light.

All: Lord, stay with us.

2.

Jesus is received by His friends in Bethany and is anointed by Magdalene

Simon: Welcome, Rabbi. How happy I am that you have accepted my invitation and you blest my house with your visit. My friends, you are all welcome.

Christ: Simon, peace be on this house! – Friend Lazarus!

Lazarus: Lord of my life.

Magdalene: Rabbi!

Martha: Welcome!

Christ: God's blessing upon you!

Martha: Master, I wish to serve you.

Magdalene: Would you allow me also to show my love and gratitude?

Christ: Do whatever you wish.

Simon: Best of masters, come under my roof. Food and drink are ready. Come too, my friends.

Christ: Then let us, beloved disciples, accept thankfully the gifts bestowed on us by the Father in heaven through Simon, his servant. Alas, Jerusalem, I wish you would welcome my arrival as much as my friends do here.

Lazarus: Your enemies are waiting to see whether you will go to Jerusalem on the day of the festival. They are watching out for your downfall.

Peter: Lord, you are safe here. Stay in the peace and safety of this house until the storm which will rise against you has passed.

Christ: Get thee behind me, Satan! Peter, you are not conscious of what belongs to God, only what belongs to man. The Son of Man has not come to let himself be served, but has come to serve and to give his life as a ransom for many.

Magdalene: Rabbi! (She anoints Christ)

Christ: Mary!

Thomas: What a lovely perfume.

Bartholomew: That is pure, precious oil of nard.

Thaddeus: Such honour has never before been shown to our Master.

Judas: Why such expense? The oil could have been sold and the money given to the poor.

Christ: What are you saying to each other? Why do you criticise what she has done only from love and gratitude?

Judas: What a waste – to pour out such a precious ointment.

Christ: Friend Judas, look at me.

Judas: I know that you do not like unneccessary expense. The ointment could have been sold and the poor could have been helped. We could have gained at least three hundred denari.

Christ: The poor will always be with you, but you will not always have me. Leave her alone. She has done good work for me: she has come beforehand to anoint my body for burial. Truly I tell you: wherever in all the world the Gospel is proclaimed, what she has done will be told as her memorial. (Christ stands up.) I thank you, Simon. The Father will reward you.

Simon: Rabbi, I shall never forget what I owe to you.

Christ: Farewell to all you who live in this hospitable house. Never again shall I stay in your peacefull town, dear, quiet Bethany. My disciples, follow me.

Peter: Lord, go where you will, but not to Jerusalem.

Christ: I am going where the father calls me, Peter. If it pleases you to remain here, then stay.

Peter: Lord, wherever you stay, there I stay too. Where you go, I will go too.

Christ: Come then.

Simon: Are you really going up to Jerusalem?

Magdalene: I have a foreboding of terrible things. Friend of my soul, my heart – my heart will not leave you.

Christ: Arise, Mary. The night is approaching, but take comfort, early in the morning you will see me again. (To everyone) Dear ones, wherever I am, I bear you in my heart, and wherever you are, my blessing will be with you. Farewell.

3.

Jesus takes leave of His mother Mary

Mary: Jesus my son, I hurried after you to see you once again.

Christ: Mother, I am on the way to Jerusalem.

Mary: To Jerusalem? I carried you into the temple there in my arms to present you to the Lord.

Christ: Mother, the time has now come to fulfil that which my Father requires of me.

Disciples: Pray to the Father that He will let this hour pass by.

Magdalene and Martha: He will hear you.

Christ: My soul is troubled. What shall I say? Father, save me from this hour? But it is for this hour that I have come into the world.

Mary: O Simeon, Simeon, venerable old man. What you once prophesied to me will now be fulfilled: "A sword will pierce your soul!"

Christ: Mother, it is the Father's will.

Mary: I am the handmaid of the Lord. What He inflicts on me I will bear. But I ask you one thing: let me suffer with you and go to death with you.

Christ: You will suffer with me, with me you will fight in my final conflict with death, but then will also celebrate with me my victory. Therefore take comfort.

Mary: O God, give me strength, that my heart break not. My Son, I will go with you to Jerusalem.

The women: We too will follow you.

Christ: Stay with our friends in Bethany for now. (To the women) I commend to you my Mother and all those who accompanied her here. (To Mary and her companions) After two days you may all go together to Jerusalem to attend the great day of the festival there.

Mary: As you wish, my Son.

Christ: Mother, Mother! Receive the thanks of your Son for the love and motherly care which you have shown me during the years of my life. My Father calls me. Farewell.

Mary: My Son, where shall I see you again?

Christ: There, where the words of the scripture are fulfilled: "He was led like a lamb to the slaughter, and He opened not his mouth."

Mary: Jesus, my Son, my Son!

The women: Merciful God!

John: What misery awaits us all!

Christ: Do not lose the first struggle. Hold firmly to me.

ACT III

Jesus' Last Journey to Jerusalem
Preparation for Betrayal by Judas

Bass solo: *Awake, all mankind, awake, all nations!*
Recognise him, the Lord, who leads you to salvation.
O do not hesitate! In him God is near us!
Turn to your redeemer.

Chorus: *O you men and people all,*
Return to your God.
But do not despise, mocking Him,
The warning call of grace,
So that in days to come
The anger of the God most high
Should not be poured over you
In full measure.

Prologue

People of God, behold, your Saviour is at hand.
The long-promised One has come.
O hear Him, follow His leading.
He will bring you blessing and life.

Chorus: *O you men and people all, you sinners, hear God's word:*
If you wish to find mercy,
Clear the corrupting element
Of sin from your hearts.

Passion

1.

Jesus' sorrow for Jerusalem

John: See, Master, Jerusalem!

Matthew: There is the temple. How magnificent!

Christ: Jerusalem, Jerusalem! That you should know it on this day, which is a day of peace! But now it is hidden from your eyes. Jerusalem, how often I wanted to collect your children together, as a hen collects her chicks under her wings. But you did not want this.

Peter: Master, why are you so sad?

Christ: Peter, the fate of our city touches my heart.

John: Lord, tell us, what will be its fate?

Christ: See, the time will come when its enemies will raise a rampart all round it, close it in from all sides and harry it. The people and children within its walls will be dashed to the ground and not one stone will be left upon another.

Judas: Tell us, when will this happen? And what are the signs by which people will see that all this will be fulfilled?

Christ: Take care that no one leads you astray. Many will come and say, "I am the Messiah", and they will lead many astray. Be watchful and have no fear when wars break out near at hand and far away. This must happen, but it is not yet the end. People will rise against people and nation against nation, and there will be famine and earthquakes in many places, and this is only the beginning of the affliction! You will be handed over, tortured and killed, the whole world will hate you because you believe in me. Then many will come to grief and will hate each other and betray each other. False prophets will arise in hordes, godlessness will spread and love among you will become cold. But those who remain steadfast until the end will be saved. Now the time has come when the Son of Man will be delivered up to men and they will kill Him.

John: Rabbi, I beg you, leave the city so that there is no opportunity to carry out the dreadful deed.

Peter: Or go and reveal yourself in your glory.

Philip: Throw down your enemies.

Judas: And set the Kingdom of God among men.

Christ: My way has been marked out by my Father – and the Lord says, "My thoughts are not your thoughts, and my ways are not your ways." Today is the first day of unleavened bread, on which the law ordains us to keep the Passover supper. Both of you, Peter you and John, go ahead and prepare the Passover lamb so that we can eat it in the evening.

2.

Jesus' concern for Judas

Christ: My disciples, come with me for the last time to my Father's house. Today you can all still come with me, but tomorrow...

Judas: Rabbi, if you really wish to leave us, first take measures for our future provision. See here, there is not enough even for one more day.

Christ: Judas, do not worry more than you need.

Judas: How good it would have been now to have the price of that wasted oil, three hundred dinari! How long we could have lived on that without worry!

Christ: You were never short of anything and, believe me, none of you will ever be short of anything at any time. Friend Judas, take care that the tempter does not overcome you.

Judas: Who will worry if I do not? Do I not keep the purse for everyone?

Christ: Yes, you do, but I fear...

Judas: I also fear that this will soon be empty and will stay empty.

Christ: Let us go on. I desire to go into the house of my Father.

3.
Judas doubts

Judas: Shall I go with Him? I am not very keen to do so. His great deeds led us to hope that He would restore the kingdom of Israel, but now He speaks of departure and death and consoles us with mysterious words about a future which is too far away and too obscure for me. "Blessed are the poor! Blessed are the powerless – the Kingdom of God belongs to them. They shall inherit the earth." I am tired of believing in this and of hoping. With Him, the only prospect is of living in continual poverty and misery and, instead of sharing with Him, as we expected, in His glorious kingdom, now perhaps we will even be persecuted and imprisoned. I shall go away in good time. I wished to share His kingdom of glory with Him, but it does not appear. And what does appear is horror and poverty. Who wants to share that with Him? Not I, not I!

4.
Temptation of Judas

Dathan: Judas! This is a favourable opportunity, he is alone. He seems to be greatly perplexed – I must try everything to win him over. Friend Judas!

Judas: Who calls me?

Dathan: A friend. Have you suffered some misfortune?

Judas: Who are you?

Dathan: Dathan, your friend, your brother.

Judas: You?

Dathan: At least, I would like to be. How is the master? I too would like to join His company.

Judas: His company?

Dathan: Are things not well with Him? Have you left Him? Tell me.

Judas: If you can keep quiet?

Dathan: You can be sure of that, my friend.

Judas: Things are not well with Him. He says himself, His last hour has come. I shall leave Him. He will bring us all to disaster. I am the keeper of the purse, but see how matters stands here. Is this how a master cares for those who are his?

Dathan: The situation looks bad.

Judas: He always says to us, do not worry about tomorrow. But if anything happens to Him today, we shall be as poor as beggars. Only today He permitted the most senseless extravagance, when a foolish woman thought she would do him honour. When I made a remark about it, I was given reproachful looks and words.

Samuel: And yet you can still be on good terms with Him? Friend, I should think it is high time for you at last to care about your future yourself.

Judas: That is precisely what I think. But where can I find a way to make a better living?

Dathan: You need not look far! The path to your fortune is before your very eyes.

Judas: Where? How?

Samuel: A large reward! Who can earn it more easily than you?

Ptolomeus: Anyone who can give information on where Jesus of Nazareth is staying the night will receive a substantial reward.

Judas: No, I can't do that! I won't do that!

Ptolomeus: Brother, do not throw your good fortune away.

Dathan: Just think, the reward is not the end of it, the High Council will continue to look after you. Who knows what you will become!

Samuel: My friend, agree.

Dathan: Come, Judas, we will take you to the High Council immediately.

Judas: For the moment I must follow the Master. I must find out everything first in order to be sure.

Dathan: Then we will go on ahead to the High Council and say that you will come later.

Judas: In three hours you will find me in the temple street.

Dathan: Brother! One man –

Judas: One word!

ACT IV

The Last Supper:
Jesus Dedicates Himself to the New Covenant in Bread and Wine

Prologue

Before the godlike Friend goes to His sufferings,
He gives Himself to those who are His
For the nourishment of their souls
On their earthly pilgrimage.

Ready to offer Himself, He institutes a sacrificial feast,
Which through all centuries, to the end of time
Shall proclaim to all men
His love.

Once long ago the Lord miraculously filled
Israel's children with manna in the desert,
And made their hearts rejoice
With the grapes from Canaan.

But Jesus offers us
A better feast. Out of the mysteries
Of His body and blood
Mercy and bliss flow for us.

Tenor solo:
*The hour now draws near
And fulfilment now begins,
Of all which through the prophets
The Lord made known to mankind.*

*"In such sacrifices", says the Lord,
"I no longer take pleasure.
I will no longer receive offerings
From their hands.*

*I establish for you a new feast",
Says the Lord, "and everywhere
Throughout the whole world there shall be
An offering in this covenant."*

1. Biblical prefiguration

With manna the Lord saves His People Israel in the Desert (Exodus 16, 1-31)

Tenor solo:
*The miracle in the Sinai desert
Points to the feast of the new covenant.*

Chorus:
*Good is the Lord, good is the Lord!
He satisfies the hungry people
With a new food
In a miraculous way.*

*But death swept away many
Who ate the bread in excess
In the desert of Sinai.*

*When worthily enjoyed
The holy bread of the new covenant
Preserves the soul from death.*

2. Biblical prefiguration

The Lord gives Israel a foretaste of the Promised Land with the grapes of Canaan (Numbers 13, 1-27)

Chorus:
*Good is the Lord, good is the Lord!
Once He gave to His people
The best juice of the vine
From Canaan.*

*But this gift of nature
Was intended by God's will
For the needs of the body only.*

*The holy wine of the new covenant
Will be His Son's own blood
To quench the thirst of the soul.*

*Good is the Lord, good is the Lord!
In the new covenant He gives
His flesh and blood in the upper room
At the feast in Salem.*

The Passion

1.

Jesus washes His disciples' feet and celebrates with them the feast of the lamb

Christ: How I have longed to eat this Passover lamb with you before I suffer, for I tell you, never again shall I eat it until the time when it finds its fulfilment in the Kingdom of God. Father, I thank you for this drink from the vine. Take it and share it among yourselves; for I tell you, from this moment I shall drink from the fruit of the vine no more until the time when the Kingdom of God comes.

Some of the disciples: Master, is this your last Passover feast?

Christ: I shall drink a new wine with you in the Kingdom of God, as it is written: "You shall drink from the fountain of eternal life."

Peter: Rabbi, when this kingdom appears, how will the places be divided?

James the Elder: Which of us will rank highest?

Thomas: Or will each have his own dominion assigned to him?

Bartholomew: That would perhaps be best, then there would be no more strife amongst us.

Christ: I am still with you and you are quarrelling about who shall have the first places! Yet here am I among you like a servant. You are the men who have stood firmly by me in my time of trial, and now I vest in you the kingship which my Father vested in me. You shall eat and drink at my table in my kingdom and on thrones as judges of the twelve tribes of Israel. But take heed, kings lord it over their subjects, and those in authority are called their country's benefactors. Not so with you. On the contrary, the highest among you must bear himself like the least, the formost of you like a servant.

Some disciples: What does he mean to do?

Christ: Peter, give me your foot.

Peter: You, Lord, will wash my feet?

Christ: You do not understand now what I am doing, but one day you will.

Peter: I will never let you wash my feet!

Christ: If I do not wash you, you are not in fellowship with me.

Peter: Then, Lord, not my feet only, wash my hands and head as well.

Christ: A man who has bathed needs only to wash his feet, then he is altogether clean. You are also clean, though not every one of you. You call me "Master" and "Lord", and rightly so, for that is what I am. Then if I, your Lord and Master, have washed your feet, you also ought to wash one another's feet. I have set you an example, you are to do as I have done for you. I shall not be with you much longer. But so that remembrance of me never fades among you, I will leave you an eternal remembrance which will be with you always. I tell you, a new covenant is beginning which I establish today in my blood, as the Father told me to do, and this covenant will last until everything is fulfilled. Praise be to you, our God, King of the World, who has created the fruit of the earth. Take this, this is my body, which is given for you. Do this in remembrance of me.

Chorus:
*Lord Jesus Christ, you yourself appointed
Your last supper
On that night, when the agony of death
Pierced your holy heart.
You took care to give comfort
And strength, you yourself
In pain of death and agony of soul.*

Christ: Praise be to you, our God, King of the World, who has created the fruit of the vine. Take this and drink, all of you, for this is the cup of the new covenant in my blood, which is shed for you and many others for the forgiveness of sins. As often as you do this, do it in remembrance of me.

John: Lord, I shall never forget your love! You know that I love you.

Chorus: *You have left us a glorious gift*
With your flesh and blood.
You said, "Take this. What I do here
You do too, in remembrance of me."
But it is to be not only a memorial –
It shall be a means of grace,
To give us your worth.

Peter: This holy feast of the new covenant shall always be celebrated by us in this way.

Matthew: And as often as we celebrate it, we will remember you and your love.

Christ: My disciples, dwell in me and I will dwell in you. As the Father has loved me, so I have loved you. If you heed my commands you will dwell in my love. But - - shall I tell you? He who will betray me sits with me at the table.

Some of the disciples: What? A traitor among us?

Peter: Is that possible?

Christ: Truly I tell you, one of you will betray me.

James the Younger: Master, one of us twelve?

Christ: Yes, one of you twelve. There is a text of scripture to be fulfilled: "He who eats bread with me will raise his foot against me."

James the Younger and Simon: Who is the faithless one?

Matthew: You know that it is not I, Master.

James the Elder and Younger: Say his name openly, the traitor!

Thomas: I would sink into the earth for shame, if it were I!

Thaddeus: Rabbi, is it I?

Judas: Is it I, Master?

John: Lord, who is it?

Christ: It is the man to whom I give this piece of bread when I have dipped it in the dish. The Son of Man is going the way appointed for him in the scriptures. But alas for that man by whom the Son of Man is betrayed! It would be better for that man if he had never been born.

(He gives Judas the piece of bread.) Do quickly what you have to do. (Judas leaves the room).

Thomas: Why is Judas leaving the room?

Christ: Now The Son of Man will be glorified, and in Him God will be glorified!

2.

Jesus' farewell discourse

Christ: For a little longer I am with you; then you will look for me, but where I am going you cannot come.

Peter: Lord, where are you going?

Christ: Where I am going you cannot follow me now, but one day you will.

Peter: Why cannot I follow you now? I will lay down my life for you.

Christ: Will you indeed lay down your life for me? Simon, Simon, Satan has been given leave to sift all of you like wheat. I have prayed for you that your faith may not fail. When you have been converted, you must lend strength to your brothers. Tonight, you will all fall from your faith on my account; for it stands written: "I will strike the shepherd down and the sheep of his flock will be scattered."

Peter: Everyone else may fall away on your account, but I never will. Lord, I am ready to go with you to prison and to death.

Christ: Truly, I tell you, Peter, this night before the cock crows twice, you will disown me three times.

Peter: Even if I must die with you, I will never disown you!

Christ: Now begins the time of trial, and I tell you: the scripture says, "He was counted among the outlaws", and these words must find fulfilment in me. Let us now stand and say the prayer of thanks.

Christ and the disciples:
"Praise the Lord, all peoples.
Magnify the Lord, all nations,
For the power of His grace rules over us;
The faith of the Lord is eternal."

Christ: Children, why are you so sad and why do you look at me with such concern? Set your troubled hearts at rest. Trust in God always; trust also in me. There are many dwelling-places in my Father's house, and I am going there on purpose to prepare a place for you. I shall come again and receive you to myself, so that where I am you may be also.

I will not leave you bereft; I am coming back to you. Now when I go away I shall ask the Father and He will send you support for all times – the Spirit of the truth. It will teach you everything and remind you of everything I have told you.

Peace is my parting gift to you, my own peace, such as the world cannot give. Keep my commands.

This is my command, love one another as I have loved you. All shall recognise by this that you are my disciples, if you love one another. I shall not talk much longer with you, for the Prince of this world approaches. He has no rights over me; but the world must be shown that I love the Father, and do exactly as He commands; so, come, let us go!

ACT V

The Betrayal of Jesus

Prologue

See the false disciple now joins
The open enemies and a few pieces of silver
Efface all love and loyalty
From his impious heart.

Without a conscience he goes
To make a shameful bargain;
For him, the best of teachers can be sold
For a traitor's reward.

The same spirit hardened the sons of Jacob,
When they, without mercy, sold their own brother
For a pitiful price into the hands
Of foreign traders.

Where the heart worships the idol of money,
Every more noble feeling is deadened;
Honour can be sold, and with it a man's word,
Love and friendship.

Bass solo: *What shudders run through all my limbs!*
Where do you go, Judas, in your frenzy?
Is it you who will sell
The Master's blood? Do you not think of the penalty?
Thunder and lightning, crash down,
Crush this evildoer!

"One of you will betray me",
Said the Lord at the meal.
Led by greed to evil deeds,
One man runs from the supper,
And this one, holy God,
Is Judas Iscariot.

Chorus: *Oh turn back from the path of sin!*
Do not do that evil deed!
But no, deaf and blind with greed
Judas hurries to the High Council
And repeats in the Sanhedrin,
What once happened in Dathan's field.

Biblical Prefiguration

Joseph is sold by his brothers (Genesis 37, 23-28)

Contralto solo: *"What will you offer for this boy?"*
Said Joseph's brothers there:
"How much will you give us?"
Quickly they give away their brother's
Blood and life for a profit
Of twenty pieces of silver.

"What will you give?" – "What will be my reward?"
Says Iscariot also, "if I betray
The Master to you?"
For thirty pieces of silver
He makes his blood bargain and Jesus is
Sold to the High Council.

Chorus: *What this scene shows us,*
Is a true image of the world.
How often have you sold and betrayed
By evil deeds your God also!
Here you curse the brothers
Of a Joseph and also a Judas,
And yet you take your own paths;
For envy, greed and brothers' hate
Unceasingly destroy
Man's peace, joy and prosperity.

The Passion

1.

Jesus is to be sold for the price of a slave

Caiaphas: What joyful news, assembled fathers! The false prophet from Galilee will soon be in our hands. Dathan has won over one of his companions who will deliver him to us and lead us to the place where he spends the night. They are both already here and are only waiting to appear before the High Assembly.

Some Councillors: Let them be called in.

Caiaphas: (to Josaphat) Yes, call them! Firstly I would like to hear your advice on the reward to be given to the man for his deed.

Nathaniel: The law of Moses gives as an indication. You know, of course: it says a slave is worth thirty pieces of silver.

Amron: Still a good payment for a false Messiah.

2.

Judas agrees to deliver up Jesus

Dathan: High Priest! I bring here a man who is willing to deliver the Galilean into your power.

Caiaphas: (to Judas) Do you know this man who gives himself out to be the Messiah?

Judas: I have been one of His followers for a long time and I know where He is accustomed to stay.

Caiaphas: What is your name?

Judas: I am called Judas Iscariot.

Some voices: We have often seen him with Him.

Caiaphas: So you would be prepared to deliver Him to us?

Judas: Upon my word!

Caiaphas: Have you any reason for doing this?

Judas: My friendship with Him cooled long ago. Now I have broken with Him completely.

Caiaphas: How did that happen?

Judas: There is nothing to be expected from staying with Him. And besides, I have decided once again to keep to lawful authority. It seems to me still the best thing. However, what will you give me if I deliver Him to you?

Caiaphas: Thirty pieces of silver! And they shall be counted out for you immediately!

Judas: (hestitates)

Dathan: Hear, Judas! Thirty pieces of silver! What a sum to win!

Nathaniel: If you do your work well, we shall not forget you so soon.

Ezekiel: You may still become a rich and esteemed man!

Judas: I am satisfied.

Caiaphas: Archelaus, bring the thirty pieces of silver from the treasury now and count them out in front of him.

Nicodemus: (stands up) Will you make such a godless bargain? And you, you despicable man, are you not ashamed to sell your Lord and Master? Is your best friend and benefactor for sale for thirty pieces of silver?

Joshua: Judas, do not be dissuaded by this jealous man.

Archelaus: Take the thirty pieces of silver and be a man!

Judas: You can rely on me.

Saras: But it must be before the festival.

Judas: The best opportunity is now. This very night he will be in your hands. Give me some armed men so that he is surrounded and every means of escape is barred to him.

Annas: The temple guard shall go with you.

Caiaphas: It would be advisable for some members of the Council to go along.

Councillors: We are all willing.

Caiaphas: Perhaps Nathan, Josaphat, Dathan and Ptolemeus.

All four: With pleasure!

Caiaphas: Judas, how will the men recognise your Master in the dark?

Judas: They must bring torches and lanterns. I will then give them a signal.

Rabinth: Excellent, Judas.

All: Excellent!

Judas: I will go ahead. When everything has been spied out, I will fetch the armed men.

Dathan: Judas, I shall not leave your side until this work is done.

Judas: I will await your men at the Bethphage Gate.

3.

The High Council decides on the death of Jesus
Some members of the Council oppose the decision

Caiaphas: All goes exactly as we wish. But now, fathers, what shall be done with this man when he is in our power?

Zadok: Throw him into the deepest dungeon!

Caiaphas: Which of you will guarantee that his supporters do not cause an insurrection among the people to free him? None of you, I see! Therefore, as High Priest, I say it is better that one man should die than that the whole nation should perish.

Archelaus: God himself has spoken through his High Priest.

Nathaniel: Now it has been spoken!

All at once: (except Nicodemus and Joseph) Yes, he must die!

Nicodemus: Fathers, am I permitted to speak?

All: Yes, speak!

Nicodemus: Has this man's death sentence been pronounced before he himself has been heard, before there has been an investigation and before witnesses have been examined? Is that just? Are such proceedings worthy of the fathers of the people of God?

Nathaniel: What! Are you accusing the High Council of injustice?

Zadok: Do you know the regulations of our holy law?

Nicodemus: Yes, I know the law of Moses as well as you, and I know that no judgement may be pronounced until after witnesses have been duly examined!

Joshua: Is there any need for examination and witnesses here? Have we not been witnesses often enough of his lawless speeches and acts?

Nicodemus: Yes, you are accusers, witnesses and judges all at one and the same time! Not only you, but I also heard the speeches of the man from Nazareth, they are of great power! His words and deeds are worthy of belief and admiration, but not disdain and punishment.

Caiaphas: What do your words reveal? Admiration for the false teacher? Do you believe in Moses and nevertheless wish to defend what the law condemns?

Ezekiel: What business have you here, traitor to the High Council?

Joseph of Arimathea: I must agree with Nicodemus. Jesus has not been proved guilty of any deed for which he would deserve death, nor will it be possible to prove any such deed. He has done nothing but good.

Caiaphas: Joseph, you too? Does not everyone know that he desecrates the Sabbath? That he misleads the people by seditious speeches? That as a deceiver he performs his supposed miracles only with the aid of Beelzebub, the King of Demons? That he gives himself out to be God, although he is only a man?

All: Do you hear?

Joseph: Yes, of course! Envy and jealousy have twisted his words and slandered his most charitable actions. His deeds have given witness that he is from God.

Nathaniel: Ha, now we know you! You yourself have been a secret follower of the Galilean for a long time. Now you have thrown off your mask!

Annas: So we have betrayers of the holy law among us? Has the tempter spread his net as far as this?

Caiaphas: Why are you here, you renegades? Go and run after your Prophet, so that you can see him before he is condemned, because it has been irrevocably decided that he must die.

All: He must die, that is our decision!

Nicodemus: I curse this decision! I will have no part in this shameful judgement of blood.

Joseph: I too will leave this Council, where innocence is murdered. I swear before God, my heart is pure.

4.

Preparations for the condemnation of Jesus

Joshua: We should be glad that we have got rid of the traitors. Now we can speak openly.

Caiaphas: Nevertheless, brothers, it will be necessary for us to sit in judgement on this man, question him and let witnesses appear against him in accordance with our law.

Archelaus: The law prescribes two or three witnesses.

Samuel: They will be available, I will supply witnesses.

Caiaphas: So far as carrying out the sentence is concerned, the safest thing for us would be if we could arrange for the Governor to condemn him to death.

Nathaniel: Yes, that is what we must try to do.

Caiaphas: Now, circumstances will show what must be done. For the moment, let us separate. But be prepared at any time to return here immediately if I call you. There is no time to lose! Our decision is taken, he must die.

ACT VI

Jesus' Agony and Capture on the Mount of Olives

Prologue

As Adam struggles, pressed down by life's burden,
With exhausted strength, in the sweat of his brow,
    To atone, alas, for his own guilt,
      So likewise is the Saviour oppressed by the guilt of others.

Engulfed in a sea of infinite sorrow,
His head bowed down to the ground with the heavy burden,
    The sweat of blood covering His face,
    He fights His fiercest struggle on the Mount of Olives.

The disciple Iscariot, his loyalty forgotten,
Brings near the minions of the law,
    Infamously misusing the token of love,
    To betray Jesus to his executioners.

Joab was likewise treacherous to Amasa;
With a false expression he pressed
    The kiss of friendship on his cheek,
    And into his body the pointed dagger!

Tenor solo: *See, Judas took the bread*
At the last supper
With the worst conscience –
And Satan at once possessed him.
"What you have to do", said the Lord,
"Judas, do it quickly!" – and he
Hurried from the supper room
To the High Council
And sold his Master.
The most terrible of deeds
Is soon done.
Today, this very night
Judas will betray Him.

Chorus: *All would then go with Jesus*
To see him suffer endure and die!

1. Biblical Prefiguration

Adam's suffering as a consequence of sin: "In the sweat of your brow you shall eat your bread until you return to the soil." (Genesis 3, 17-19)

Contralto solo: *Oh what labour, what heat*
Must father Adam bear!
See, a stream of sweat falls
Over his brow and face.

Chorus: *This is the fruit of sin;*
God's curse oppresses nature!
Therefore she yields her fruit
Only sparingly, though with bitter sweat
And arduous labour.

Contralto solo: *So too it is hard for our Saviour*
When He struggles on the Mount of Olives
So that a stream of bloody sweat
Is forced from all His limbs.

Chorus: *This is the struggle of sin!*
The Lord struggles for us,
He struggles in His own blood,
Conquers – and with firm courage drinks
The cup of suffering empty!

2. Biblical Prefiguration

Joab pretends to give his brother a kiss of friendship and stabs him (2. Samuel 20, 7-10)

Bass solo: *The evil deed near the rocks of Gibeon*
Is now repeated by Judas, Simon's son!

> *You rocks of Gibeon!*
> *Why do you stand without dignity,*
> *Once the proud boast of the Holy Land,*
> *As if covered in a veil of mourning?*
> *Speak, I adjure you, what deed was done?*

Chorus:
> *Flee, wanderer!*
> *This blood-drenched spot*
> *Is accursed. Here long ago fell Amasa,*
> *Pierced by an assassin's hand,*
> *Trusting the greeting of holy friendship*
> *Deceived by a false brotherly kiss.*
> *"Oh", calls our voice;*
> *"Curse on you!"*
>
> *The rocks lament for you;*
> *The blood-drenched earth takes revenge.*
>
> *Be silent, rocks of Gibeon, and learn with horror*
> *What we see on the Mount of Olives.*

Bass solo:
> *Judas gives the Son of Man,*
> *With a hypocrite's greeting*
> *And with a false kiss,*
> *Into the hands of the impious*
> *For the vile gain of money,*
> *Oh you rocks of Gibeon!*

Chorus:
> *Cursed be the man who betrays,*
> *Who pretends love with dissembling face,*
> *Who approaches with the Judas kiss of innocence,*
> *But means betrayal in his heart.*
> *"Curse him!" shall sound from the rocks*
> *"Curse him!" the echo will say.*

The Passion

1.

Judas leads the temple guards to the Mount of Olives

Judas: Take care. The attack must be unexpected, then there will be no possibility of defence.

Temple guard: And if they attempt it, they will feel the effect of our weapons.

Judas: Do not worry. He will fall into your hands without a sword thrust.

Josaphat: How shall we recognise your master in the dark?

Judas: I will give you a signal. Listen, the one whom I shall kiss is he.

Kosam: Good, this sign will make us sure.

Ptolemeus: Do you hear? We will know him by the kiss.

Judas: Now let us hurry on. It is time; we are not far from them.

Josaphat: Judas, if we succeed in this, you will be given great honour.

2.

Jesus comforts His disciples and prays for them

Christ: In very truth I tell you, you will weep and mourn, but the world will be glad. Though you will be plunged in grief, your grief will turn to joy; for I shall see you again. Then you will be joyful, and no one can rob you of your joy... I came from the Father and have come into the world. Now I am leaving the world again and returning to the Father.

Peter: See, now you are speaking plainly and without parables.

James the Elder: Now we can see that you know everything.

Thomas: By this we believe that you have come from God.

Christ: Do you believe now? See, the hour is coming when you are all scattered, leaving me alone. Yet I am not alone, because the Father is with me.

Yes, Father, the hour is come! Glorify your Son, that your Son may glorify you! I have completed the work which you gave me to do. I have made your name known to the men whom you gave me in the world. Holy Father, keep them in your name. Sanctify them in the truth. Your word is truth.

But I pray not only for my disciples, but also for those who through their words put their faith in me, so that they may all be one, as you, Father, are in me and I in you. Father, I desire that these men, who are your gift to me, may be with me where I am, so that they may look upon my glory. For you loved me before the world began.

Sit here while I go and pray. Pray that you do not fall into temptation. But you, Peter, James and John, go with me.

James the Elder: What is going to happen to our Master? I never saw him so sad.

Peter: Not for nothing has He prepared us for this hour and urged us to pray.

Philip: We will sit here and wait for Him.

Thomas: Yes, that is best.

Christ: My heart is ready to break with grief. Stop here and stay awake with me. I will go a little further away to gain strength by calling on the Father.

James the Elder: Why does the Master keep us separate from each other today?

Peter: We were witnesses of His transfiguration on the mountain. But now what shall we see?

3.

Jesus prays in agony and is strengthened by the angel

Christ: So this hour shall pass over me, the hour of darkness! But this is why I came into the world. – – Father, my Father, if it is possible – and all things are possible to you – let this cup pass me by. – – Yet not as I will, but as you will. – – Simon, are you asleep?

Peter: See, Rabbi, here I am.

Christ: Could you not keep awake for one hour with me?

Peter: Forgive me, Lord, I was very tired, but now I will keep awake with you.

James and John: Sleep overcame us.

Christ: Stay awake and pray with me.

All three: Yes, Lord, we will stay awake and pray.

Christ: The spirit is willing, but the flesh is weak. Abba, my Father, your commands are holy. You demand this sacrifice. – Abba! Father! – But if it is not possible for this cup to pass me by without drinking it, your will be done. Holiest! Let me fulfil your will. –
Are your eyes still so heavy that you cannot keep watch? My disciples, I find no consolation with you either.
How everything now grows dark around me. The dread of death encompasses me. The burden of God's judgement weighs upon me. Oh, the sins of mankind press me down. Oh, the fearful burden, the bitterness of this cup! – My Father, if it is not possible for this hour to pass me by, your will be done! – Your holiest will! – Father! – Your Son! – Hear him!

Angel: You are my servant –
You will be great and exalted!
Bear the sickness of mankind!
Take their sufferings on yourself!
The spear will pierce you for their crimes,
You will be crushed for their sins!
Heal them through your wounds!
The Lord delights in His broken servant,
He saves Him who gives His life in atonement!

Christ: Yes, your will be done, Most Holy!

4.

Judas betrays Jesus with a kiss – Jesus is taken prisoner

Christ: Are you still asleep?

Peter: What is the matter, Rabbi?

Christ: The hour has come! The Son of Man is delivered into the hands of the sinners. Get up and let us go. See, my betrayer approaches.

Andrew: What does this mob want?

John: And see, Judas at the head of them!

Judas: Hail, Rabbi!

Christ: Friend, what have you come here for? Will you betray me with a kiss? – Who are you looking for?

Temple guard: Jesus of Nazareth.

Christ: I am he.

Some of the Temple guard: Woe to us! What is this?

Disciples: A single word from Him will hurl them down.

Christ: Stand up. Once again, I ask, who are you looking for?

Temple guard: Jesus of Nazareth.

Christ: I have – told you, I am he. So if you are looking for me, let these others go.

Selpha: Go, seize him!

Peter and James the Elder: Master, shall we use our swords? (Peter strikes the servant Malchus)

Malchus: Oh! My ear!

Christ: Peter! Put up your sword. All who use the sword shall die by the sword. Shall I not drink the cup which my Father has given me? Or do you suppose that I cannot appeal to my Father, who would at once send to my aid more than twelve legions of angels? But how then could the scriptures be fulfilled, which say that this must be? You have come out with swords and cudgels against me as if I were a bandit. Day after day I sat teaching in the temple, and you did not lay hands on me. But this is your hour and the power of darkness. See, here I am!

Selpha: Seize him and tie him up, so that he cannot escape!

Nathan: You are responsible to the High Council for his not escaping.

Some of the Temple guard: He will not get away from us.

Josaphat: We will go on ahead into the city. The High Council awaits our arrival.

Nathan: First to the High Priest, Annas. Take him there!

Selpha: We will follow you.

Josaphat: Judas, you are a man, you have kept your word.

Judas: Did I not tell you, he would be in your power today?

Ptolemeus: You have put the High Council in your debt.

Temple guard: Come on with you!

Selpha: Let us hurry!

Some of the Temple guard: Forward, or we will drive you with blows.

ACT VII

Interrogation and Ill-Treatment of Jesus by Annas

Prologue

Behold the Saviour!
From one court to another He is dragged
    Meeting with abuse
    And ill-treatment on every side.

For a freely spoken word addressed to Annas
A miscreant rewards Him with a blow from his brutal fist
    In His divine face
    In order to gain favour.

Micaiah also receives the same ignominious reward,
For revealing the truth to Ahab, the King;
    One of the lying prophets
    Gives him a blow on the cheek.

Truth often reaps hatred and persecution only;
But whether you see or avoid its light –
    Finally it will triumph
    And break through the darkness.

Chorus:
> *The painful battle has begun,*
> *Begun in Gethsemane.*
> *Oh sinners! Take it well to heart,*
> *And never forget this scene!*
> *This was done for your salvation,*
> *What now you see on the Mount of Olives.*

Biblical Prefiguration

Micaiah the prophet receives a blow for telling King Ahab the truth (1. Kings 22, 1-36)

Tenor solo:
*He who openly speaks the truth
Receives a blow in the face.
Micaiah, who ventured to tell the truth aloud,
Received a blow in the face.*

*"Oh, King, if you wage war on Ramoth,
You will be defeated.
Do not believe what is prophesied,
By those devoted to the service of Baal.*

Bass:
*Do not believe the flatterers' words.
Hear the voice of one sent by God,
Who will not deceive you, Ahab!"
For these words, in anger,
A liar struck his face.*

Chorus:
*Liars, hypocrites, flatterers gather
Roses and laurels without effort.
Only the truth must bend down,
For the truth never flatters.*

The Passion

1.

The High Priest Annas awaits the prisoner Jesus

Annas: I can find no rest until this criminal is in our hands.

Esdras: They cannot be much longer.

Annas: I can see nothing in Kidron Street. There is nothing to be heard or seen. Esdras, go to the Kidron Gate und see whether they are coming.

Esdras: As the High Priest commands!

Annas: It would be a great misfortune if we did not succeed in arresting the Galilean.

Misael: I do not doubt we shall be successful.

Annas: Every minute waiting seems more like an hour. Listen, I hear footsteps. Yes, someone is coming.

Sidrach: Esdras is coming.

Annas: He must have good news or he would not hurry so.

Esdras: Greetings to our High Priest! Everything went according to plan. The Galilean has been arrested.

Annas: Happy news! Praise be to the God of our Fathers!

2.

Judas learns that Jesus must die

Four Councillors: Fortune and salvation to the High Priest!

Nathan: The wish of the High Council is fulfilled.

Annas: So our plan has succeeded!

Selpha: High Priest, here is the prisoner, as you ordered.

Annas: Judas, your name will have an honoured place in our annals. The Galilean shall die even before the festival.

Judas: Die? Die?

Annas: His death is decided.

Judas: I did not wish that!

Annas: That does not concern us, he is in our power.

Judas: I did not deliver him to you for that.

Ptolemeus: You delivered him to us, what happens next is our affair.

Judas: What have I done? Is he to die? No, I will not have that!

The Councillors: Whether you like it or not, he must die!

3.

Jesus is interrogated and struck

Annas: Was he alone taken prisoner?

Balbus: Yes, his followers scattered like frightened sheep.

Selpha: Incidentally, Malchus nearly lost his life.

Annas: How, what happened?

Selpha: One of the Galilean's followers struck at him with his sword and cut off his ear.

Annas: There does not seem to be any wound.

Balbus: The false prophet has apparently put it on again by magic.

Annas: Why do you not say something yourself, Malchus?

Malchus: I cannot explain it. A miracle has happened to me.

Annas: Has the deceiver bewitched you too? Tell me, by what power have you done this?

Christ: (is silent)

Selpha: Answer when your superior asks you a question.

Annas: Speak, give an account of your disciples and the doctrine you have spread throughout the land, by which you have misled the people.

Christ: I have spoken openly to the world. I have always taught in the synagogues and the temple, and I have never said anything in secret. Why do you ask me? Ask those who heard what I said to them. They know what I said.

Balbus: (strikes him in the face) Is that the way to answer the High Priest?

Christ: If what I said was wrong, then prove it. But if what I said was right – why do you strike me?

Annas: Do you still defy us, even though your life is in our hands? Take him away.

Balbus: Just wait, your defiance will soon pass.

Annas: The High Council must question him and pronounce the sentence this very morning.

4.

Jesus is brought before the High Priest Caiaphas

Arphaxad: Have they finished questioning him?

Selpha: His defence was not successful.

Balbus: It earned him a good slap across the face.

Selpha: Take him and let us hurry to the High Priest Caiaphas.

Temple guard: Away with him! Hey, get a move on!

Balbus: Your followers want to proclaim you King!

Selpha: Caiaphas will announce your elevation to you.

Temple guard: Do you hear? Your elevation between earth and sky!

ACT VIII

The High Council Sentences Jesus to Death
Judas' Torments of Conscience
Betrayal and Remorse of Peter

Prologue

Before His judges
The Lord stands in silence; patiently
He listens to all their accusations, even
    The sentence of death.

As Naboth was once persecuted innocently,
Condemned as a blasphemer by false testimony,
So He too, whose only offence is truth,
    Love and acts of charity.

But soon you will see Him encircled by inhuman henchmen,
Delivered to rude mockery,
    Scornfully ill-treated amidst wild laughter.

In patient Job, who in his deepest affliction
was covered with mockery, even by his friends,
You see prefigured our Saviour's
Sufferings borne for us.

Bass solo:
> *How my heart bleeds!*
> *The Most Holy stands before the court.*
> *He must bear the malice of sinners,*
> *Betrayed and insulted, bound and beaten.*
> *Who would not shed a tear?*
> *Dragged away from Annas to Caiaphas –*
> *What will He have to suffer there!*
> *See here this new scene of suffering!*

1. Biblical Prefiguration

The innocent Naboth is condemned to death by false witnesses (1. Kings 21, 1-16)

Chorus:
*"Naboth must die! He dared to blaspheme God
And to revile you, oh King:
May he be wiped out from Israel!"
This is the brazen call of slanderers
Hired by the wicked Jezebel
To swear a false oath.*

*Alas, by death is punished a crime
Which Naboth never committed.
His vineyard is then given over
By rascals to the King.*

*Again they all stand together
Against Jesus before the court
Until a false sentence is pronounced
To condemn the innocent.*

*You mightly rulers of the world,
Set up for the welfare of humanity,
Do not forget in carrying out your duty
The invisible Judge!
Before Him all men are equal,
May they be rich or poor,
Noble men or beggars,
Justice is His only purpose!*

2. Biblical Prefiguration

Pious Job, sorely tried, is mocked for his faith (Job 2, 9 ff.)

Bass solo:
*See a Job groaning in pain!
Ah, who would not weep at the sight!
His wife and his friends deride
And mock him to His face.
Behold the man!*

Chorus: *Yet patiently he bears the torment,*
Surrounded by derision and mockery,
He trusts confidently in his God,
He utters no sound of complaint.
Behold the man!

Behold Jesus, how silently He bears
The rudeness that insults and strikes Him.
Behold the man!

Oh give Him compassion, when you see Him standing,
Humbled before you
In deepest shame, the man of pain!
Behold the man!

The Passion

1.

Judas suffers torments of conscience

Judas: Uneasy forebodings make me restless! Annas' words, "He must die", torments me wherever I go! It would be terrible if they killed my Master – and I the cause of it! If the Master had wished to save Himself, He would have let them feel His power a second time in the Garden of Gethsemane. As He did not do it then, He will not do so now. They shall have the money back, the blood money! They must give me back my Master! You unjust judges! I will have nothing to do with your decision! I will have no share in the blood of the innocent!

2.

The High Council prepares the trial of Jesus

Caiaphas: I awaited the morning dawn with impatience, venerable fathers. Everything is ready for the trial. Samuel has brought the necessary witnesses.

Nathanaiel: It must all be over before our adversaries can join together in a revolt.

Caiaphas: That is also my opinion. Samuel, bring the witnesses in – and you, Solomon, see that the prisoner is brought before us.

3.

Jesus is accused by witnesses and condemned to death by the High Council

Selpha: Noble High Priest! Here is the prisoner, as you commanded.

Caiaphas: Bring him nearer so that I can look in his face and question him.

Selpha: Step forward and honour the head of the High Council.

Caiaphas: You are accused of inciting the people to disobey the law, despising the inherited doctrine of the fathers, violating the divine commandment to keep the Sabbath holy, and even of indulging in blasphemous words and deeds. Here stand honourable men who are prepared to verify the truth of these accusations with their testimony. Hear them, and then you may defend yourself if you can.

Nun: I can testify that this man stirred up the people by publicly calling the scribes "hypocrites" and "rapacious wolves in sheeps' clothing", and he told the people not to obey their writings.

Eliab: Yes, I heard that too.

Caiaphas: What do you say to this? Nothing? Have you nothing to say in reply?

Gad: I have seen him on friendly terms with publicans and sinners, going into their houses to eat with them.

Eliab: I have heard from trustworthy persons that he even spoke to Samaritans and even stayed with them for days at a time.

Nun: I was a witness of how he healed the sick and afflicted on the Sabbath. For example, he commanded a man he had healed to carry his bed home on the Sabbath, and another to wash in the pond of Siloah.

Eliab: I saw that too.

Caiaphas: What do you have to say to these statements?

Christ: (is silent)

Gad: You have taken it upon yourself to forgive sins, which is for God alone to do. Therefore you have blasphemed God.

Eliezer: He said, "I will destroy the temple of God and build a new one in three days, which will not be built by the hand of man."

Caiaphas: So you have boasted that you have superhuman, divine power? These are serious accusations, and they are lawfully proven, deny them if you can. -- I see that you think you can save yourself if you keep silent.

Annas: If you are the Messiah, tell us.

Christ: Even if I do tell you, you will not believe me, and if I ask you a question, you will not answer it, nor will you release me.

Caiaphas: Listen, Jesus of Nazareth, I the High Priest, abjure you by the living God. Tell us, are you the Messiah, the Son of God, who is praised on high?

Christ: Yes, I am. But I tell you, from now on you will see the Son of Man sitting at the right hand of God, and coming on the clouds of heaven.

Caiaphas: (tearing his robe) He has blasphemed God! Do we need any more witnesses? You yourselves heard the blasphemy. What do you think?

Councillors: He deserves to die!

Caiaphas: He has been condemned to death by the High Council. But it is not I, not the High Council, - God's law itself pronounces the judgement on him. You teachers of the law, I summon you to answer; What does the holy law say concerning blasphemers of God?

Nathaniel: Any man who blasphemes the name of the Lord shall die. The whole community shall stone him.

Caiaphas: Accordingly, judgement is pronounced on this Jesus of Nazareth.

The High Council: He is guilty of disobeying the law, profaning the Sabbath and blasphemy, and accordingly deserves to die.

Caiaphas: We shall now have the death sentence confirmed by the Governor. We must produce the Galilean to Pilate as an enemy of the state and tell him that this Jesus wants to be the Messiah, the King of the Jews. Take the prisoner away for the present.

Councillors: Yes, take him away!

Annas: God grant that soon the time will come that will deliver us from him for ever.

Councillors: God grant it!

4.

Judas laments his betrayal

Judas: Is it true?

Archelaus: How dare you push your way uncalled into our assembly?

Judas: You have condemned my Master to death?

Archelaus: Get out! You will be called if you are wanted.

Judas: I must know! Have you condemned Him?

Councillors: He must die!

Judas: Woe betide me! I have sinned! I have betrayed innocent blood, but you are murdering innocence.

All: Be quiet, Judas.

Judas: No more rest for me, and none for you! The blood of innocence calls to heaven.

Caiaphas: What confuses your soul? Speak, but with respect.

Judas: You wish to deliver to death that man who is free of all guilt. You must not do it. I appeal. You have made me into a traitor! Your accursed pieces of silver!

Annas: You yourself made the offer and agreed on the sale.

Josaphat: You have received what you asked for.

Judas: I will have no more! Give up the innocent man!

Archelaus: Control yourself, you fool!

Judas: I demand back the innocent man! My hands shall be clean of that just man's blood –

Archelaus: What? You infamous betrayer, are you trying to lay down laws for the High Council? Your Master must die, and you have delivered Him to His death.

All: Yes, he must die!

Judas: Must He die? Am I a traitor? Have I delivered Him to death? Then tear me to pieces, you devils from the deepest hell, destroy me! Here, you have your accursed blood money!

Caiaphas: Why did you let yourself get carried away to do a deed which you did not consider beforehand?

Judas: Then let my soul be doomed, and my body burst asunder, and you – you shall all perish with me!

Caiaphas: A madman!

Annas: I had a presentiment of this.

Aman and Oziel: It is his own fault.

Caiaphas: Let him atone now for what he has himself done. He has betrayed his friend, we pursue our enemy. We must now bring him before Pilate's judgement seat so that he confirms the judgement before the festival and has it carried out.

Archelaus: Perhaps a few of the Councillors could go to him beforehand and request him to hear the matter without delay.

Caiaphas: You yourself would be best, Archelaus, then Dariabas and Rabinth. You go on ahead. We and the other Councillors will follow as soon as the Governor has agreed.

5.

Jesus' disciples in fear

Philip: We ought to have been more watchful. Judas took us completely by surprise with the temple guards. Where is Peter?

Andrew: I saw him and John following the guards a long way behind. Their concern for Jesus will ensure that they venture as far as the High Priest's palace.

Thomas: Judas chose the moment for betrayal well – the night when everyone is celebrating the Passover feast and we did not have time to inform our friends.

Andrew: I dare not go into the street. Nowhere is one safe from spies.

Thomas: If only this night were over.

Philip: In this night the Prince of Darkness rules! This night everything will be fulfilled!

Andrew: What will happen to Jesus?

Philip: The High Priests are capable of condemning Him to death. "He was led like a lamb to the slaughter, and He opened not His mouth." Lord, save us, we shall perish.

Andrew: He reminded us to pray and have faith – now we must trust in the Lord and His word.

Thomas: Let us go! I hear a noise and people shouting.

6.

Peter denies his Master

Agar: Men, come in here with your guard.

Sara: It is warmer in here.

Melchi: Hey, comrades, come in here. It is better if we camp here.

Arphaxad: I can put up with this! We always stand outside and freeze.

Panther: Agar and Sara, bring a fire and some wood to put on afterwards.

Agar: Yes.

Temple guard: The trial seems to be taking a long time.

Melchi: Yes, yes, it may be a long while before all the witnesses have been questioned.

Panther: And the accused will no doubt summon up all his eloquence to talk his way out of it.

Arphaxad: But it will not help him. The Councillors have been too greatly offended by him.

Agar: Here is warmth for you.

Sara: And wood and firetongs!

Arphaxad: Many thanks, you girls.

Panther: Take care the fire does not go out.

Agar: John, are you here too? Come in, you can warm yourself here. You can find a little space for this young man here, can't you, men?

Levi and Abdias: Come here!

John: Agar, I have a friend with me. Can he come in too?

Agar: Where is he? Let him come in, why should he stand outside in the cold? Well, where is he?

John: He is at the gate but will not venture to come in.

Agar: Come in, don't be afraid!

Abdias: Yes, come over here and warm yourself.

Levi: We won't hurt you!

Arphaxad: There is nothing to be heard or seen of the prisoner still.

Temple guards: How much longer will we have to wait here?

Panther: They will probably condemn him to death.

Arphaxad: I wonder whether they will look for his disciples too.

Panther: It is not worth the trouble. When the Master has gone, they will not be seen here in Jerusalem any more.

Arphaxad: At least the one who cut off Malchus' ear should receive a proper punishment.

Agar: I have been watching you a long time. If I am not mistaken, you are one of his disciples. Yes, yes, you were with Jesus, the Nazarene!

Peter: Me? I do not know him, and I don't know what you mean.

Sara: Yes, he was with Jesus of Nazareth.

Levi: Yes, You are one of his disciples.

Peter: No, I certainly am not. I do not even know the man.

Abdias: You are lying. Of course you were with the Galilean, I have often seen you with him.

Peter: I really do not know what you want of me. What is this man to me?

Levi and Abdias: Now you have betrayed yourself. You too are a Galilean, your dialect proves it.

Peter: God is my witness that I do not know this man of whom you speak.

Melchi: What are you saying; Did I not see you this evening in the Garden of Gethsemane, when one of them cut off my cousin Malchus' ear?

Temple guard: Get ready, the prisoner is being brought out!

Selpha: He has been condemned to death.

Temple guard: Oh poor king, what will become of you now?

Selpha: Come now, comrades, we must guard him.

Levi: Yes, we can amuse ourselves with him instead of being bored.

7.

The temple guards mock Jesus as a false prophet and king

Levi: Is this throne not too humble for you, great king?

Melchi: We greet you, Messiah! But sit more firmly, otherwise you could fall off.

Levi: You are a prophet, aren't you? Tell us, did he strike you?

Abdias: Was it me?

Levi: Well, can't you hear?

All: He is deaf and dumb! A fine prophet!

Abdias: Oh, what a shame! Our king has fallen from his throne.

Levi: What shall we do? We no longer have a king!

Melchi: You deserve pity. Once you were such a great miracleworker, and now so weary and feeble.

Abdias: Come, let us help him back on to his throne.

All: Rise up, mighty king. Receive our homage again.

Dan: Well, how is it with our new king?

All: He says nothing, and makes no prophecies.

Dan: The High Priest and Pilate will make him talk. Caiaphas has sent me; it is now time to take him to the Governor.

Selpha: Make ready, comrades.

Levi: Get up, Galilean. You have been king long enough.

All: Away with you. Your kingdom is at an end!

8.

Peter regrets his betrayal and hopes for mercy

Peter: Oh, best of masters! How far have I fallen! I am a weak, miserable man. Three times have I disowned you, my Friend and Teacher, you for whom I promised to go to death. What shameful disloyalty! Lord, if you will still have mercy for me, mercy for one who has been unfaithful, then give it to me. Hear the voice of a repentant heart. See, the sin has been committed. I cannot undo it, but I will lament and atone for it. Never more will I leave you! Lord, you will not cast me out, you will not spurn my bitter remorse? No, you will forgive me! This is my hope, and all the love of my heart shall be yours from this moment on, and nothing, nothing shall ever separate me from you again.

ACT IX

The Dispair of Judas

Prologue

Why does Judas wander bewildered,
Tortuted by the anguish of his conscience?
    Blood guilt weighs down his soul.

Lament Judas, what you have done.
Meekly hope for mercy,
    The gate of salvation is still open for you.

Bitter remorse torments him,
In the darkness no ray of hope.
    "Too great – too great is my sin!"
    He cries with Cain, his brothers murderer.

Like him – restless, agitated, unreconciled –
Driven to the depths of wild despair.
    This is sin's final reward,
    It drives one toward such fate.

Tenor:
"Woe to the man", said the Lord
"Who will betray me.
It would be better for him
If he had never been born!"
And this woe of which Jesus spoke
Now follows the footsteps of Judas.

Chorus:
He shall not miss the full reward of his offence.
The blood he sold cries aloud.
Driven to raving by his conscience,
Lashed by the rage of all furies,
Judas wanders about restlessly
And finds repose nowhere.

Biblical Prefiguration

Cain, murderer of his brother, finds no refuge from his tormented conscience (Genesis 4,8-16)

Contralto solo: *Likewise Cain flees, but where to?*
You cannot flee from yourself!
In yourself you carry hell's tortures.
And though you hurry from place to place,
They swing their scourges steadily.
Wherever you are, there they are also,
You can never escape the pain.

Chorus: *Let this be a warning to sinners.*
For if punishment does not come today,
Heaven can still wait,
And the double weight
Fall on their heads tomorrow.

The Passion

Judas despairs and ends his life

Judas: Where can I go to hide my shame, to get rid of the torture of my conscience? I have sold my Master, delivered Him up to ill treatment, to the most painful death of a martyr. What a detestable betrayer I am! Where is another man on whom such guilt rests?

How good He was always to me! How He admonished me, and warned me, when I had already decided on the shameful betrayal. And I, this is how I have repaid Him!

Accursed greed! Only you have led me astray, made me blind and deaf. Greed it was which Satan seized me with to draw me into the abyss. As an outcast, hated and despised everywhere, even by those who led me astray branded as a traitor, I wander about on my own with this fire burning within me!

Yes, there is still one! Oh, if only I could see His face once again! I would cling to Him. But this one man is in prison and perhaps already dead – through my fault! I am the reprobate who has brought him to prison and death! Woe betide me, there is no hope for me. My crime is so great, it cannot be made good by any repentance. He is dead – and I am His murderer. Unhappy hour, in which my mother brought me into the world! Am I to drag out my wretched life any longer? Bear these tortures within me? No, not one step further! Here will I end my accursed life. Let the miserable fruit hang on this tree! Ha, come, you serpent, wind about my neck and strangle the betrayer.

ACT X

Jesus before the Roman Governor Pilate and King Herod

1.

Jesus, bound, is surrendered to Pilate

Temple guard: Death to you, you false prophet!

Selpha: Drive him on!

Levi: Move on, your journey will not last much longer!

Temple guard: Out to Calvary!

Caiaphas: Silence now, we will have our arrival announced.

2.

The Councillors assemble before Pilate

Quintus: What do all these people want?

Archelaus: The High Council has assembled.

Quintus: I will notify my master immediately.

Caiaphas: You members of the High Council, if you have at heart our religion, our honour and the peace of the whole country, heed this moment. It will decide our fate. Be firm in your resolution.

All: We shall not waiver.

3.

The High Council demands that Pilate also condemns Jesus to death

Caiaphas: Governor, representative of the great Emperor of Rome!

All Councillors: Hail and blessing on him!

Caiaphas: We have brought this man, Jesus by name, before your judgement seat and we ask your permission for the sentence pronounced by the High Council to be carried out.

Pilate: What is your accusation against him?

Caiaphas: If he had not been a great malefactor, we would not have brought him to you.

Pilate: Well, of what crimes is he guilty?

Caiaphas: He has gravely offended our holy law in many ways.

Pilate: Then take him, and judge him according to your law.

Annas: He has already been judged by the High Council, which has found that he should die.

Caiaphas: But we are not allowed to execute anyone. For this reason we sent a request to Caesar's representative for the judgement to be carried out.

Pilate: How can I judge a man without knowing his crime and being sure that he deserves death? What has he done?

Archelaus: The death sentence on this man was pronounced by the High Council after close examination of his crimes. Therefore it does not seem necessary for Caesar's representative to trouble himself with any further investigations.

Pilate: What are you thinking of? You dare to presume that I, Caesar's Governor, should be a blind instrument for carrying out your decisions? I must know what law he has broken, and in what way.

Caiaphas: We have a law, and according to that law he must die, because he has called himself the Son of God.

Amiel: We all heard this blasphemy from his own lips.

Annas: Therefore we must insist that he suffers the ordained penalty of death.

Pilate: No Roman can condemn a man to death for such talk as this. If you have no other crime of which you can accuse him, I shall not consider granting your request.

Caiaphas: He is guilty of serious offences against Caesar too.

All: He is a rabble-rouser, an insurgent.

Pilate: I have certainly heard of a man, one Jesus, who goes about the country teaching and performing unusual deeds, but I have never heard anything about a rebellion. How, and in what way, is he supposed to have caused a rebellion?

Nathaniel: He gathered crowds of people about him, thousands of them, and only a few days ago he made a triumphant entry into our holy city of Jerusalem, surrounded by such a crowd, and had homage paid to him as the King of Israel.

Pilate: I know that, but it did not give rise to a rebellion.

Caiaphas: Is it not rebellion when he tells the people not to pay taxes to Caesar?

Pilate: What proof have you of this?

Caiaphas: Is it not enough if he proclaims himself to be the Messiah, the King of Israel? Is he not setting the people on to rebel against Caesar?

Pilate: I admire your enthusiasm for Caesar's esteem. – Do you hear what serious accusations they bring against you?

Christ: (is silent)

Caiaphas: See, he cannot deny them.

Ezekiel: His silence is a confession of his crimes.

All: So judge him!

Pilate: I will question him alone, in confidence. Perhaps he will speak to me and answer my questions. Take him into the forecourt. My soldiers will take charge. But you must consider once again whether your accusations are justified.

Joshua: Everything has already been examined and verified.

Archelaus: This will create further delay.

Caiaphas: Do not lose courage. Our perseverance will gain the victory.

4.

Pilate questions Jesus and asks Him about His kingdom

Pilate: You have heard the accusations. Give me an answer. Where are you from?

Christ: (is silent)

Pilate: Will you not answer me either? Do you not know that I have power to crucify you or release you?

Christ: You would have no power over me if it were not given to you from above. Therefore he who has delivered me to you has the greater sin.

Pilate: Really, a good answer! Are you the King of the Jews?

Christ: Is that your own idea, or have others suggested it to you?

Pilate: Am I a Jew like you? Your people and the high priests have handed you over to me. They accuse you of having proclaimed yourself King of the Jews.

Christ: My kingdom is not of this world. If my kingdom were of this world, my disciples would have fought for me so that I would not have fallen into the hands of my enemies. But my kingdom is not of this world.

Pilate: So you are a king?

Christ: "King" is your word. My task is to bear witness to the truth. For this, I was born; for this I came into the world, and all who are not deaf to truth listen to my voice.

Pilate: What is truth?

5.
Pilate's wife is frightened by a dream about Jesus

Quintus: My lord, Claudius has just come to inform you of an urgent request from your wife.

Pilate: Let him in. For the moment, take the prisoner into the entrance hall. – What have you to say to me?

Claudius: Your wife earnestly begs you to have nothing more to do with that just man who has been accused before your judgement seat. Last night she had a dream and suffered great fear and terror on his account.

Pilate: Who is just!? Claudius, go and tell her not be frightened by dreams. I know how to judge!

6.
Pilate consults his staff

Pilate: I find this trial a burden!

Silvus: The high priests pretend that Caesar's esteem is very close to their hearts.

Mela: I think the accusation is based on other grounds.

Pilate: I think as you do. I cannot believe that this Jesus has criminal plans in His mind. I will on no account be party to fulfilling the wishes of the High Council. Silvus, let the high priests appear once more, and the accused be led out of the judgement hall.

7.
Pilate refuses to accept jurisdiction and refers Jesus' case to Herod

Pilate: Here you have your prisoner again. He is not guilty.

Annas: Not guilty? We have Caesar's word that our laws shall be upheld. How is it possible that anyone who treads these laws underfoot can be not guilty?

Councillors: He is guilty of blasphemy.

Caiaphas: Is He not guilty before Caesar if He violates what Caesar has guaranteed us?

Pilate: I have already told you; if He has broken your law, punish Him according to your law, provided you have the right to do so. I at least cannot pronounce a death sentence on Him, because I find nothing in Him which, under the law of Rome, merits death.

Caiaphas: If anyone on his own authority declares himself king in a province of Caesar, is he not an insurgent? Does he not deserve the penalty for high treason?

Pilate: If this man has called himself a king, that is far from being sufficient reason for me to condemn Him for high treason. In Rome every wise man is called a king. I am not aware that He has incited a rebellion.

Nathaniel: Is it not creating a disturbance when the whole people is stirred up by Him, when He wanders through the whole of Judea with His preachings – from Galilee all the way to Jerusalem?

Pilate: What do you mean? Did He come from Galilee?

Some priests: Yes, He is a Galilean.

Archelaus: His home is in Nazareth, in the territory of King Herod.

Pilate: If that is the case, I have no jurisdiction in this matter. Take Him to King Herod. He is here in Jerusalem for the festival anyway. My guards shall take your prisoner to him.

Caiaphas: Away then to King Herod! With him we shall find more sympathy for our holy law.

Annas: Even if a thousand obstacles stood in our path, the blasphemer shall receive His deserved punishment.

All: Yes, and today!

8.

Jesus before Herod

Herod: Let the priests enter.

Caiaphas: Mighty King!

The priests: Hail and blessings be upon you from the Almighty!

Caiaphas: The High Council has condemned a transgressor to death for blasphemy and has brought Him before the King for cornfirmation of the lawful sentence.

Annas: And may it please the King to approve the judgement of the High Council.

Herod: How can I be a judge in foreign territory? Take your prisoner to the Governor.

Caiaphas: Pilate has sent Him here because He is a Galilean and is therefore your subject.

Herod: Who is this man?

Some priests: Jesus of Nazareth.

Herod: Jesus of Nazareth? Strange! Pilate sends Him to me? Grants me leave to act as judge in his province?

Naason: It seems that the Governor wishes to show you his favour once again, high King.

Herod: It shall be to me a token of his new friendship. -- (To Jesus) I have heard that you can see into the secrets of men's hearts and perform deeds which go beyond the bounds of nature. Therefore let us have proof of your miraculous power. Change the water in this glass into ruby red wine, as you are once said to have done at a wedding ceremony. Or make it suddenly grow dark in this room. - I see very well; he knows nothing and can do nothing.

Naason: With credulous people it is easy to pretend to do something, but He fails miserably before the wise and mighty King.

Manasse: If you really can do something, why is your wisdom silent here?

Herod: He is a simple man whose head has been turned by the applause of the people. Let Him go.

Caiaphas: Oh King, do not trust this cunning schemer.

Annas: If He is not removed, even your throne is in danger. Not long ago He proclaimed Himself as king.

Herod: He? As king? He could be recognised as the king of fools at the best. I will present Him with an old royal mantle as a present.

Some priests: Not this – it is death He deserves!

Herod: Once you said to my emissaries: "On the third day I shall be at my destination." What was that supposed to mean? And you added: "I shall go up to Jerusalem, for it cannot be that a prophet should perish outside Jerusalem." – Do you give no answer to this?

Christ: (remains silent)

Herod: Do you give no answer to this?

Caiaphas: King, think of your duty to punish the betrayer of the law.

Herod: What has He done then?

Archelaus: He has profaned the Sabbath.

Nathaniel: He has even blasphemed God!

All priests: Therefore the law finds that He should die!

Herod: Put this mantle on Him! Let Him play His part as the king of fools in this royal mantle. Present Him to the people so that they may admire Him to their hearts' content. In my opinion He is a fool and He is not capable of the crimes of which you accuse Him.

Annas: Oh King, I fear you will regret it if you judge Him so leniently.

Herod: My decision stands; He is a fool, and must be treated as a fool. Let Pilate dispose of Him in accordance with his official duty. Send him greetings and friendship from King Herod. Friends, this Jesus is not a prophet like John. John spoke with wisdom and strength which had to be admired. But this man says nothing. Come, let us go.

9.

Jesus is brought back to the goverrner Pilate

Caiaphas: Time is running short, the day moves on. Now we must do our utmost to achieve our purpose today, before the festival. If Pilate does not give judgement as we wish, we will threaten to appeal to Caesar. (Pilate enters) We bring the prisoner once more before your judgement seat and now most earnestly demand the penalty of death.

Pilate: You have brought this man to me as a rebel and troublemaker. Because He is a Galilean, I had Him taken to Herod, but he also found nothing in Him which deserves death. On the contrary, he put Him in a mocking mantle and sent Him back to us. Therefore I will have Him flogged for the offences of which you accuse Him, but then I will release Him.

Annas: That is not enough!

Caiaphas: Our law does not prescribe flogging, but death, for blasphemy.

All councillors: Yes, death!

Pilate: I have heard your judgement, but now I will hear the voice of the people of Jerusalem. They will soon gather here in any case to beg for the release of one prisoner for the Passover festival, in accordance with ancient custom. Then we shall see whether the people also condemn this Jesus and demand His death. You know this Barabbas, who is in prison for robbery and murder. I shall let the people choose between him and Jesus of Nazareth. I will release whichever the people choose.

All: Release Barabbas!

Amiel: Put the other on the cross!

Pilate: You are not the people! They shall decide. For the moment, I will have this man flogged. The soldiers will take Him away and flog Him in accordance with the law of Rome.

10.

Caiaphas asks the Counsillors to stir up the crowd

Caiaphas: Pilate puts his faith in the voice of the people. We too put our faith in the people. Go out into the streets of our city and summon our followers to come here. Try to win over the waverers by the power of your words and by promises. But frighten the followers of the Galilean away, so that none dares to show his face here.

Councillors: We will soon come back.

Dathan: Each at the head of an enthusiastic crowd!

Caiaphas: We will meet in the Sanhedrin Street.

Annas: From all the streets of Jerusalem we will then lead the excited people before the courthouse.

Archelaus: If Pilate wants to hear the voice of the people, let him!

11.

Jesus is flogged and crowned with thorns like a mock king

Caspius: He has had enough now.

Sabinus: What sort of a king is this? No sceptre in his hand, no crown on his head?

Domitius: That can be arranged!

Caspius: Wait!

Milo: He must become a real king.

Sabinus: You shall be royally equipped.

Caspius: But sit down, so that we can crown you king! See here, this is a magnificent attire for a false king.

Milo: Is it not? You had not expected such honour?

Caspius: Come, let us put your coronation robe around your shoulders.

Milo: Here is a splendid crown for your head, with many sharp thorns.

Domitius: Come, brothers, help me!

Sabinus: And here is your sceptre!

All: We greet you, mighty king!

Mela: The prisoner must be taken into the judgement hall immediately.

Domitius: You have disturbed us in the middle of paying homage!

Milo: Into the judgement hall! Stand up, you will be shown to the people as a spectacle.

Sabinus: There will be rejoicing among the people when their king appears before them in such splendour!

Lictor: Take him and lead him away!

ACT XI

Jesus is sentenced to Death on the Cross

Prologue

A picture of misery, the Redeemer stands.
Pilate presents him without pity.
    Behold the man!
    Have you all no mercy?

No, without mercy you call:
To the cross, to the cross with him!
    But for Barabbas
    Demand pardon.

How differently before the people of Egypt once
Stood Joseph! Songs of joy surrounded him.
    As the saviour of Egypt
    He was presented with all festivity.

But you rage around Him, the Saviour of the world,
Unresting and unceasing
    Until the judge
    Cries: so take Him and crucify Him!

Tenor solo: *O, see the King, see Him crowned*
                      In scorn, but what a crown!
                      And what a sceptre in His hand!
                      See Him arrayed in purple.
                      In scorn bedecked in a crimson mantle.
                      Is that the festal garb of a king?

Chorus: *Behold the man!*
                      Where in Him is a trace of deity?
                      The sport of cruel hangmen.
                      Behold the man!

Bass solo: *Pilate presents him without pity.*
Behold the man!
Joyous shouts ring before Joseph.

1. Biblical Prefiguration

In contrast to Jesus, Joseph is acclaimed by the people as their saviour (Genesis 41, 37-43)

Chorus: *Loud shall it ring through Egypt.*
"Long live Joseph, All honour to him!"
And a thousand times it shall resound:
"Father and friend of Egypt is he!"
And all unite, both great and small,
In our joyful exultation!

Soprano solo: *You are Egypt's pride and joy,*
Fame which it has never known before,
To you, Joseph, Egypt today brings
Homage and exultation.

Chorus: *Long live Joseph, fine and noble!*
A thousand times shall it resound:
"Father and friend of Egypt is he!"
And all unite, both great and small
In our joyful exultation!

2. Biblical Prefiguration

One sacrificial animal is released but the other is slaughtered in expiation of sins (Leviticus 16, 1-34)

Contralto solo: *This is the sacrifice of the old covenant*
As the Highest ordained.
Two goats were presented,
Then lots were cast on them,
To decide which the Highest chooses.

Chorus:	*O Eternal One, take the victim's blood,* *Be reconciled to your people.*
Bass and contralto:	*In the new covenant the Lord* *No longer requires the blood of goats.* *He requires a pure sacrifice.* *A lamb, pure of all blemish,* *Must be the offering of this covenant.*
Bass solo:	*The Lord demands His own Son;* *Soon He comes – soon falls – And soon He bleeds!*
Chorus:	*O Israel! O people of God!* *The blood of the lamb purifies you* *Of all guilt;* *It gives you forever surely* *God's grace.*

The Passion

1.

The multitude, stirred up by the High Priests, rejects Jesus

Nathaniel: Moses, your prophet, calls upon you to save his holy law!

People: We are and remain the sons of Moses and his teaching. You are our fathers, we pledge ourselves to you!

Annas: Follow the advice of the High Council, it will save you.

Ezekiel: Shake off the yoke of the tempter, throw it off!

People: We will know nothing more of him, we follow you. We wish to be free of this false teacher.

Caiaphas: The God of your fathers will receive you back again.

People: Long live the High Council! Long live our teachers and priests!

Annas: And may the Galilean die!

Caiaphas: Come, let us hurry to Pilate.

Nathaniel: Let us demand His death!

People: Away to Pilate! The Nazarene shall die!

Caiaphas: He corrupted the law. He despised Moses and the prophets. He blasphemed God.

People: To death with the false prophet! The blasphemer must die! Pilate must have Him crucified!

Caiaphas: He will pay for His misdeeds on the cross.

People: We shall not rest until the sentence is spoken.

Caiaphas: Yes, you are still the true descendants of your father Abraham. Thank God that you have escaped from the indescribable doom which this deceiver wished to bring on you and your children.

Annas: Only the untiring efforts of your fathers have saved you from the abyss.

People: Long live the High Council! Let the Nazarene die!

Caiaphas: The Governor will give you a choice between this blasphemer and Barabbas. Let us insist on the release of Barabbas.

People: Let Barabbas go free! Let the Nazarene perish!

Annas: Praise be to you, and our fathers, who have heard our prayers!

People: Pilate must consent! We insist on it!

Caiaphas: Remain steadfast! Be impetuous in demanding the judgement.

People: We demand the conviction of the Galilean!

Servants and soldiers: Rebellion! Insurrection!

People: The Nazarene must die!

Caiaphas: Show courage! Hold out undaunted! Our just cause protects us.

People: The death penalty!

Nathaniel: Let Pilate speak the death penalty.

Pomponius: Silence! Be quiet!

People: No, we will not hold our peace until Pilate gives a righteous judgement.

Pomponius: The Governor will appear immediately.

Caiaphas: Now, may Pilate pass judgement on this blasphemer.

2.

Pilate releases Barabbas and condemns Jesus to death on the cross

Nathaniel and Archelaus: Judge Him!

People: Judge Him! Sentence Him!

Pilate: Look at that man!

High Council: To the cross –

People: Let Him die! To the cross with Him!

Pilate: So take Him and crucify Him, for I find no guilt in Him.

Caiaphas: Governor, hear the voice of the people of Jerusalem. They join in our accusations and demand His death.

People: Yes, we demand His death.

Pilate: Lead Him down, and let Barabbas be brought here from prison.

Annas: Let Barabbas live. Pronounce the death sentence on the Nazarene.

People: To death with the Nazarene!

Pilate: I do not understand you people. A few days ago you accompanied this man rejoicing through the streets of Jerusalem. Is it possible that today you call down death and destruction on Him?

The crowd: It wasn't us! We are not His disciples.

Caiaphas: They have finally realised that they were deceived by a false teacher, who presumed to call Himself the Messiah, the King of Israel.

Nathaniel: Now their eyes have been opened, because they see that He cannot help Himself, He who promised freedom and salvation to all.

Ezekiel: Israel wants no Messiah who lets himself be taken and bound and mocked.

People: Let Him die, the false Messiah, the deceiver!

Pilate: Men of Judea! It is the custom for me to release to you a prisoner at the Passover. Which of these two shall I release, Barabbas or Jesus, who is called the Messiah?

Some of the people: Free Jesus, Jesus!

Priests and people: No, not Him, but Barabbas!

Pilate: Do you not want me to give you your king?

Voices from the crowd: Set him free!

Priests and people: Away with Him! Free Barabbas!

Caiaphas: You promised to release the one chosen by the people.

Pilate: I am accustomed to keep my promises without being reminded of them. What shall I do then with the King of the Jews?

Some of the people: Free Him, He is innocent!

People: Crucify Him, crucify Him!

Pilate: What? Shall I crucify your king?

High Priests and Councillors: We have no king but Caesar.

Pilate: I cannot condemn this man, for I find no offence in Him.

People: If you release Him, you are not a friend of Caesar.

Caiaphas: He set Himself up as king.

Priests: And he who sets himself up as king opposes Caesar.

Nathaniel: And is this rebel to go unpunished?

People: It is the Governor's duty to condemn Him.

Caiaphas: Now we have truly done our duty as Caesar's subjects and delivered this rebel to you. If you disregard our accusation, at least we are free from blame. You alone, Governor, will then be responsible to Caesar for the consequences.

Annas: If there is general disquiet and revolt because of this man, we shall know where the guilt lies, and Caesar will also hear of it.

People: The matter must be brought before Caesar.

Ezekiel: They will be surpised in Rome to learn that you have given protection to a traitor.

People: You must have Him executed, otherwise there will be no peace in the country.

Pilate: What wrong has He done then?

People: Crucify Him!

Caiaphas: May I be allowed one question? Why are you so apprehensive in judging this man, whereas not long ago you had your soldiers put to death hundreds of people, without a trial and without sentence, who had only been shouting seditious words? We shall not move from this spot until you have pronounced the death sentence on Caesar's enemy.

People: Yes, we shall not move from this spot until the sentence has been pronounced.

Pilate: Bring me some water. (To Aurelius) They shall have the death sentence written out immediately. See, I wash my hands of it, I am innocent of the blood of this man. All of you, see!

Several: Blood be on us and on our children.

Pilate: Let Barabbas be set free by your demand. Take him away, outside the city gate, so that he may never set foot on this land again.

Priests and people: Now you have decided justly.

Annas: We and our children will bless this day and will speak the name of Pontius Pilate with joy and thanks.

Priests: Long live our Governor!

People: Long live Pontius Pilate!

Pilate: Bring the two murderers out of the prison. They shall be taken to Golgatha with Jesus.

Priests and people: He above all deserves death!

Chief Lictor: Won't you go? Kick them forward!

Archelaus: Ha! That is fit company for the false Messiah on His last journey.

Pilate: Today the earth will be rid of both of you and your infamous deeds. You shall die on the cross. Now let the death sentence on Jesus of Nazareth be proclaimed.

Aurelius: (reads) I, Pontius Pilate, gouverner of Judaea under mighty Ceasar, Claudius Tiberius, on entreaty by the high priests and high council; hereby pronounce the sentence of death on Jesus of Nazareth, who is accused of having incited the people to revolt, forbidden them to pay tax to Caesar, and proclaimed Himself as King of the Jews. Therefore, he shall be nailed to a cross outside the city walls and in this way put to death. Given in Jerusalem, in the 18th year of the reign of Caesar Tiberius.

Pilate: Now take Him and crucify Him.

Caiaphas: Victory is ours! Rejoice, our faith is saved!

Priests and people: Take Him to Golgotha!

People: Long live the High Council!

Priests and Councillors: Long live the faith of our fathers!

Caiaphas: Let our triumphant procession now go through Jerusalem.

Archelaus: Where are His supporters now, to call hosanna?

People: Away to Golgotha! So it will be with all who despise the law. He deserves death on the cross. It is all over with the Galilean!

Archelaus: His followers will soon scatter.

The people: This Jesus will soon be forgotten.

ACT XII

Jesus on the Way to the Cross and the Place of Execution on Mount Golgotha

Prologue

The infamous sentence of death is spoken.
Forth on His way to the place of skulls
We see Jesus staggering, laden with the
    Beams of the cross.

Isaac once carried upon his own shoulders
Wood for sacrifice to the mountain top,
Where he himself was intended for sacrifice
    By the will of the Lord.

Jesus also bears willingly the burden of the cross,
Thereon to sacrifice His sacred body,
And soon the cross will become a source of blessing,
    The tree of life.

For as the people were healed by the sight
Of the brazen serpent raised in the desert,
So also we receive consolation, blessing and redemption
    From the tree of the cross.

Chorus:
Worship now and render thanks!
He who drank the cup of suffering
Now goes to death on the cross,
And reconciles the world with God.

1. Biblical Prefiguration

Abraham is willing to sacrifice his son Isaac, who himself carries the wood for the sacrifice up Mount Moriah (Genesis 22, 1-13)

Contralto solo: *Even as Isaac himself carried*
The wood for sacrifice to Moriah,
Jesus, laden with the cross,
Staggers on to Golgotha.

Chorus: *Worship now and render thanks!*
He who drank the cup of suffering
Takes the way of the cross, crowned in thorns,
Till He reconciles God and the world.

2. Biblical Prefiguration

The bronze serpent lifted up by Moses brings salvation to those in danger of death (Numbers 21,8)

Bass solo: *Nailed to the cross,*
The Son of Man is raised aloft.
Here in Moses' serpent you see
The cross prefigured.

The people were liberated
From the venomous snakebites.
In the same way salvation and bliss
Will flow to us from the Cross.

Chorus: *Worship now and render thanks!*
He who drank the cup of suffering
Now goes to his death on the cross,
And reconciles God and the world.

The Passion

1.

Mary follows her son

Mary: What will have happened to my Son since I saw Him for the last time in Bethany?

John: If the priests could have their way, He would be alive no longer. Perhaps they have already pronounced judgement, but they dare not put it into effect without the Governor's permission. The life of one man is of little consequence to the governor, but he will not do the High Priests the favour of allowing Jesus to be executed.

Magdalene: May the Lord incline the Governor's heart to justice, that he may protect the innocent.

Mary: Who could tell me where I could see my Son again? I must see Him! But where shall I find Him?

John: The best thing would be to go to Nicodemus. We shall most likely learn from him what has happened to the Master.

Mary: Yes, let us go to him. My anxiety for the fate of my Son increases every moment.

John: Dear Mother, whatever happens, it is God's will.

2.

Jesus, bearing the cross, is led to Golgotha

People: Go on! Push him on!

Joseph of Arimathea: What is this?

People: He should die! He should die!

Agrippa: Is the load too heavy for you already?

People: Drive him on so we can get to Calvary.

Faustus: Stop! Otherwise He will collapse.

Joseph: What shall we do? With this terrible commotion, we don't dare to go into the city.

Mary: What can this noise mean? Surely it cannot concern my Son?

Joseph: A riot seems to have broken out.

John: We will wait here until the storm is over.

3.

Mary meets her Son

Priests and people: Go on! Don't let Him rest! Hit Him to make Him go.

Catilina: Your lingering will not help you, you must go on to Golgotha.

Cleopha: Those wild shouts are coming nearer!

John: It seems that someone is being taken out to Calvary for execution.

Mary: It is He! Oh God, it is my Son! My Jesus it is!

John, Magdalene and Salome: Mother, dear Mother!

Lictors: Here, take strength. Would you not like a drink? Then drive Him on.

4.

Simon the Cyrenian helps Jesus to carry the Cross

Nero: Stir yourself, you lazy Galilean!

Faustus: Collect your strength together!

Catilina: He is too feeble, someone must help.

Captain: (to Simon the Cyrenian) Come here, you have broad shoulders which can carry something.

Simon: I? I must go into the city!

Nero: No, you must help us!

Simon: I do not know –

Captain: You will know soon enough, do not refuse!

Faustus: Or you will regret it!

Simon: What do you want of me? I have committed no offence.

Captain: Silence!

Simon: Don't push me! What do I see? It is the holy man of Nazareth!

Faustus: Put your shoulders here!

Simon: For love of you I will carry it.

Christ: God bless you and yours.

Captain: Now forward! (To Simon) You follow us with the cross.

Agrippa: Now we can go faster!

Catilina: See, even the cross is taken from you!

5.

Jesus meets Veronica and the weeping women

Veronica: Oh Lord, how your face is covered with blood and sweat. Would you not wipe it?

Christ: Faithful soul, the Father will reward you.

Seophora, Rebecca and Susanna: This is how they reward you!

Judith: Is it possible? Such ingratitude!

Christ: You daughters of Jerusalem, do not weep for me, but for yourselves and your children. For the days are surely coming when they will say, "Happy are the barren, the wombs that never bore a child, the breasts that never fed one." Then they will start saying to the mountains, "Fall on us", and to the hills, "Cover us." For if these things are done when the wood is green, what will happen when it is dry?

Rachel: What will happen to us and our children?

Judith: Woe betide us!

Captain: Get back now, it is time for us to go on!

Faustus and Nero: On with you to Golgotha!

Archelaus: Are we really going on at last?

Nathaniel: The captain is much too considerate.

Priests: Do not treat Him so gently!

People: Up to Golgotha! To the cross with Him! To the Cross! Let Him bleed on the cross! We are free! Long live our fathers, death to the Galilean!

6.

Mary and the friends of Jesus go with Him on the way to Golgotha

Mary: Alas, I see Him led to death like a criminal between the other criminals! The anguish I suffer is like no other!

John: Mother, it is the hour which He foretold. It is the Father's will. I fear you will not be able to bear the sight of your Son.

Mary: How could a mother leave her child in dire need? I will suffer with Him, I will share scorn and disgrace and die with Him.

John: If your strength does not fail you!

Mary: John, do not fear for me. I have prayed to God for strength; the Lord has heard me. Let us follow them.

All: Mother, we follow you!

ACT XIII

Jesus' Suffering and Death on the Cross

Prologue

Up, pious souls, arise and go,
Burning with pain, remorse and thanks,
With me to Golgotha and see
What happened here for your redemption.
There dies the Mediator between God
And sinners, the atoning death.

Naked, only clothed with wounds,
Soon He will hang here on the cross for you.
The merciless feed their eyes
Wantonly on His torment.
And He, who thee, O sinner, loves,
Is silent, suffers, endures and forgives.

Up, pious souls, draw near the lamb,
Who freely gives Himself for you.
Behold Him on the tree of the cross.
See, hanging between murderers,
God's Son gives His blood.
And you shed not a tear for Him in return?

They hear Him pray aloud to His father
To forgive even His enemies;
And soon He sacrifices His life
So that we may escape eternal death.
A spear pierces through His side,
And opens His heart to us still more.

Bass solo: *Who can conceive of this great love,*
Which loves even unto death,
And instead of hating the crowd of murderers,
Blesses and pardons them!

Chorus: *O bring to this great love*
Your pious heart's emotion,
Upon the altar of the cross
As a great offering.

The Passion

1.

Jesus is raised on the Cross and mocked

Captain: Now get hold and raise the cross.

Catilina: Up, with all your strength!

Nero: The cross stands firm.

Captain: Now it's done.

High Council: Thanks and applause from us all!

Annas: What is that inscription? Does it call him King?

Archelaus: (reads) Jesus of Nazareth, King of the Jews! That is mockery, an affront to the High Council and the whole people.

High Council: This title must be removed. Tear it down!

Caiaphas: We dare not lay hands on it ourselves. Archelaus and Saras, go to the Governor and demand, in the name of the High Council, that this inscription be changed. Pilate should write that the Nazarene himself said, "I am the King of the Jews."

Archelaus and Saras: We will go immediately.

Caiaphas: Then request also that the bones of those who have been put to death should be broken and their bodies taken down, so that they do not stay hanging on the cross on the Sabbath.

Catilina: Now, comrades, let us divide what we have inherited. See, His mantle gives exactly four pieces. But the tunic is seamless, woven in one piece throughout. Shall we cut it up? That would be a pity.

Faustus: No, it would be better to throw dice for it.

Agrippa: Here are dice. I will try my luck. That is too little!

Catilina: If you on the cross can still do miracles, favour my throw!

Nero: Fifteen, almost enough. Now you try, Faustus!

Faustus: Yes, I must have it.

Catilina: Eighteen, that's the highest.

Agrippa: It is yours.

Archelaus: Our mission was in vain.

Saras: He would not even listen to us.

Caiaphas: Did he not give you an answer?

Archelaus: He only said, "What I have written, I have written."

Annas: Outrageous!

Caiaphas: What answer did he give you about breaking the bones?

Archelaus: He said the captain would receive orders about that.

Caiaphas: So it will remain written: King of the Jews.

Joshua: If you really are the King of Israel, come down from the cross, so that we may see and believe it.

Eliezer: You wanted to destroy the temple of God and rebuild it in three days, so now help yourself.

Caiaphas: He helped others, but He cannot help Himself.

Nun: Come down! You have said yourself, "I am the Son of God."

Annas: He trusted in God, so let God save Him now, if He loves Him.

2.

Jesus' last words and His death

Christ: Father, forgive them, for they know not what they do.

Gesmas, the thief on the left: Do you hear? If you are God's anointed, save yourself and us.

Dismas, the thief on the right: Do you not fear God either, since you have been condemned to the same punishment? We suffer justly, for we received the reward which we deserved for our crimes, but this man has done no evil. Lord, remember me when you come into your Kingdom.

Christ: Truly, I tell you, today you will be with me in paradise.

Caiaphas: Just listen! He is still speaking as if He were the Lord of paradise.

Archelaus: Has His arrogance still not left Him, although He hangs so helplessly on the cross!

Christ: Mother, see your Son! Son, see your Mother!

Mary: So, dying, you still think of your Mother!

John: May His last wish be sacred to me. You my Mother and I your son.

Christ: I am thirsty.

Captain: He is thirsty and calls for a drink.

Faustus: He shall have it. Here, drink!

Christ: Eloi! Eloi! Lama sabachtani! My God, why have you forsaken me?

Bystanders: Listen, he is calling on Elias.

Caiaphas: Now we shall see whether Elias will come to take him down from the cross of shame.

Christ: It is accomplished! Father, into your hands I commend my spirit.

Enan: What is that? The earth trembles!

Captain: Truly, this was a just man. His patience in the cruelest sufferings, His noble serenity, His loud call to Heaven shortly before His death! Truly, He was the Son of God!

Bystanders: Almighty God, we have sinned, have mercy on us.

Zorobabel: High priest, a terrible thing has happened in the temple!

Caiaphas: By Almighty God, what has happened?

Zorobabel: The curtain of the temple has been torn in two!

Priests and High Council: Frightful! Ghastly!

Caiaphas: Let us go and see what has happened.

3.

Jesus' heart is pierced

Nicodemus: Has the holy body really been thrown in the pit for criminals?

Joseph of Arimathea: Friend! Hear my plan. I will go down to Pilate and ask him to give me Jesus' body. He will not refuse. Then I will bury Him in my new tomb in the rock.

Nicodemus: Yes, do that, dear friend. In the meantime I will obtain precious ointments to prepare His body for burial.

Captain: Do not be afraid, you women. You can come nearer. No one may do you harm.

Magdalene: Oh my teacher, how my heart sorrows for you.

Quintus: On the Governor's orders, the bones of those who have been executed must be broken and their bodies taken away. It must all be done before the eve of the great feast.

Captain: It shall be done immediately. Men, get up and break the bones of those two first.

Mary: My Son, surely they will not treat your holy body so cruelly?

Magdalene: Spare Him, spare Him!

Catilina: He is already dead.

Faustus: To be sure He is dead, I will pierce His heart with my spear.

Mary: Ah!

Magdalene: Dear Mother! This thrust has pierced through your heart also.

Captain: Now take the bodies down from the cross.

Agrippa: Where shall we take them?

Captain: Into the pit for criminals, in accordance with regulations.

Mary: What a terrible word, it wounds my heart anew!

Nero: Bring ladders here!

Magdalene: So we may not even pay the last honours to our friend?

Captain: Unfortunately, it is not in my power to grant your wish.

Faustus: You climb up, I will hold it.

Catilina: And I will look after the other.

4.

Joseph of Arimathea receives the body for burial
The High Priests have the body guarded

Caiaphas: We have seen the destruction which has occurred in the temple. I hope the Galilean's corpse will soon be thrown into the pit for criminals.

Annas: See, the bodies are already being taken down.

Quintus: The Governor has sent me to ask you whether Jesus of Nazareth has already died?

Captain: See for yourself. His heart has been pierced with a spear, to make sure.

Quintus: Then I am commanded to tell you that His body has been given to this man as a present, Joseph of Arimathea.

The women: Consoling news!

Caiaphas: We will not allow Him to be buried anywhere else.

Captain: Since the body has been given to this man by the Governor, it goes without saying that he can bury it where and how he wishes. Men, we have done our duty. Let us return.

Annas: Now we must be vigilant. This deceiver in fact said, when he was still alive, "After three days I will rise again."

Archelaus: His disciples could steal the body secretly and then spread the story that He had risen again.

Caiaphas: Then the last deception would be worse than the first. Let us go to Pilate at once and ask him for men to guard the grave until the third day.

Annas: A good idea!

5.

Jesus is taken from the cross and laid in His Mother's lap

Magdalene: Now they have gone. Take comfort, beloved Mother. See, now at last we are alone with our friends. The mockery and the blasphemy have ceased.

Mary: What my Jesus suffered I have suffered with Him. Now it is accomplished, He has gone to the Father's peace. Peace and comfort have also entered my heart from Heaven.

Magdalene: Remember the words that your Son said to you when He departed from Bethany, "You will fight with me in my conflict with death, but then you will also celebrate with me my victory." – Certainly he has not gone from us forever. We shall see him again.

Cleopha: Spread out the linen for His martyred body.

Joseph: Oh holy burden, come onto my shoulders.

Nicodemus: Come, holy body, let me embrace you. How you have been torn by the fury of your enemies.

John: Here the best of sons shall rest once again in the bosom of His dearest Mother.

Mary: My Son, how your body is covered with blood and wounds.

John: From these wounds flow blessing and salvation for mankind.

Mary: Once before at Bethlehem, now at Calvary! The path which the Father marked out for you is at an end. My Son, they have driven nails through your hands and feet and pierced your heart with a spear. Your sufferings and bitter death went through my soul like a sword. But now I shall not despair; I know that on the cross you have atoned for the sins of mankind and have redeemed us all.

Funeral Song

Chorus:
All you who pass by here,
Stand still, pay heed and watch.
Where will you find A love
Which can compare to this?

ACT XIV

"On the third day He rose again according to the scripture; He asceded to heaven and sits at the right hand of the Father!"

1.

Jesus arises from the tomb

Titus: Patience, Caspius. Day is breaking now.

Caspius: (jumps up) What is that? An earthquake?

Titus: What's the matter with me, I have gone blind!

Milo: Brothers, what happened?

Caspius: Did you not see the lightning?

Titus: I saw a figure all of light, and bright as the sun!

Sabinus: I saw the light too!

Titus: See, the stone has been rolled away!

Milo: Yes, indeed, and the tomb is empty!

Sabinus: He must have arisen!

Titus: Let us hurry into the city and report what has happened here!

2.

The angel shows the women the empty tomb

Magdalene: How happy I am to pay the last tribute to our beloved teacher.

Salome: But who will roll away the big stone for us with which they have sealed the tomb?

Magdalene: See, the tomb is open, the stone has been rolled away from the entrance!

Salome: Here are the cloths in which the holy body was wrapped. It is no longer in the tomb!

Angel: Fear not, you seek Jesus of Nazareth, who was crucified. He is not here, He has arisen from the dead! He will go on before you to Galilee. You will see Him there, as He told you.

Salome: Let us hurry and bring the joyful news to His disciples!

3.

Christ appears to Mary Magdalene

Christ: Mary!

Magdalene: That is His voice! – Rabbuni!

Christ: Do not touch me. I have not yet gone to my Father. But go to my brothers and tell them that I am going to my Father and your Father, to my God and your God!

Magdalene: He has disappeared; I can see Him no longer. – But I did see Him! I heard His voice! He lives! The Divine One, the merciful friend of sinners, He who makes blessed all who believe in Him! Oh, if only I could proclaim it throughout the whole world, so that mountains and rocks, heaven and earth should re-echo:

"Halleluja, He has arisen!"

CONCLUSION

Epilogue

He is risen! Rejoice you heavenly hosts!
He is risen! Rejoice you mortals all!
>   The lion from the tribe of Judah
>   Has trodden down the head of the serpent.

The faith is firm. Most joyous hope has wakened.
In our hearts by the symbol and pledge
>   Of our own future resurrection.
>   Call in jubilation: Halleluja!

Now He ascends to the highest glory
>   Where He will gather round Him
>   All whom He has redeemed with His blood.

Where the eternal song of victory resounds:
Praise be to the lamb who was slain,
>   Joyfully united with our Saviour
>   We shall see each other again.

FINAL TABLEAU

Halleluja! Praise the conqueror of sin and death!

Chorus:
Halleluja! Overcome –
By the hero is the foes' power.
He – who slumbered only a few hours
In the gloom of the grave.
Sing to Him in holy psalms,
Strew before Him victory palms,
The Lord is arisen!
Rejoice in Him you heavens,
Halleluja, Christ is risen!

Soprano solo and chorus: *Praise to you, conqueror of death,*
Who once died on Golgotha.
Praise to you, Saviour of all sinners,
Who conquered on Golgotha.
Praise to you who on the altar
Gave your life for us.
You have purchased our salvation,
We die, to live in you.

Halleluja
praise, renown, adoration, power and glory be thine for ever and ever

"HIS BLOOD BE ON US AND ON OUR CHILDREN"

An Epilogue

In spite of being persistently urged to do so, the Parish of Oberammergau has felt unable to remove the words of the so-called blood guilt from its Passion Play. Does this mean that an opportunity for making people think has been lost – or created?

Remembrance instead of suppression
The effect these words have had throughout history is so terrible that the call to remove them from all Passion Plays is understandable. But what would be gained by erasing the memory of this bloodstained history when a saying in the Bible was misused? Should we not allow ourselves to be reminded that there is a history of guilt in tradition itself, in interpreting Bible passages with evil intent? Does it serve the cause of truth if we suppress facts and the pretended reasons for anti-Semitism among Christians?

Enough arguments have been produced both for and against leaving out the words about blood guilt. Anyone who has seen the Play knows that the production has a greater effect than the precise words of the text, whether they are shouted out by the whole crowd of Oberammergau people in front of their Pilate or whether they are uttered only by a small group, as specified by the 1984 text.

If the words were omitted, the whole scene would have to be dropped, so that there would be no more criticism. In 1990 this scene no longer contrasts a good Pilate with bad Jews. On the contrary Pilate, for whom, according to the new text, a man's life counts for little, and the Jews and we Christians are guilty, as the Prologue rightly says: "let each of us recognise his own guilt in these events."

The words explain the events

The words about blood guilt are not historical. The crowd which gathered in front of Pilate's palace early in the morning of Good Friday, perhaps a hundred strong, wanted the release of Barabbas, who had been arrested for taking part in a rebellion. They refused to ask for Jesus to be amnestied instead of Barabbas, as Pilate proposed. At the instigation of members of the High Council the crowd demanded the crucifixion of Jesus.

The words do not appear in earlier versions of the story of the Passion. They form part of the explanation which Matthew gave of Jesus' suffering. Matthew alone describes the scene where Pilate washes his hands and says, "I am not guilty of this man's blood." In Matthew's account the Gentile refuses to accept responsibility for Jesus' death and lays the blame on the Jews: "this is your doing!" This is the only place where the words about blood guilt appear. With them "the whole people" accept responsibility for Jesus' death. When they say, "His blood be on us and on our children", they mean, "We are aware of our responsibility and we accept the consequences". The words "and on our children" indicate that historical responsibility is not discharged in a single generation.

The words interpret history in the Jewish tradition

The words about blood guilt are not meant to be anti-Semitic or anti-Jewish. They are formulated in the Jewish biblical tradition and are based on the empirical wisdom of Israel. There is no other nation which has pondered upon the consequences of its own acts with such radical self-criticism, which has exposed self-deception and created awareness of responsibility to such an extent as Israel, the people of God. What Matthew wrote followed in this tradition.

He realised that the scene he added would have an explosive effect: it was not ignorant Gentiles who were mainly responsible for the death of Jesus, but members of the nation whom God had chosen for himself. Jesus was one of that nation, he was its Messiah, "the king of the Jews". As no-one went to Jesus' assistance, not even his cowardly disciples, Matthew makes the "whole people" responsible.

He spoke of this responsibility to those who shared in it, the Christian communities who believed that Jesus' death was an act of salvation and regarded God's forgiveness as the decisive turning-point in the history of the world. Matthew held them especially responsible for Jesus' death. Any future bloodshed caused or permitted by them would be a new crufixion of Jesus, who had died once and for all for everyone.

In view of our history we Christians have every reason for accusing ourselves: we also belong to the "whole people" which spoke the words of blood guilt.

The worst scandal in the history of the world
Jesus was a Jew. Anti-Semitism of any kind is directed also against him. The fact that we Christians failed to realise this for centuries shows how far removed we are from him who taught us, "It is from the Jews that salvation comes" (Jn 4,22). Christianity's most momentous sin is that it tried to separate Jesus from his people after the synagogue had already divided from the church. It was in the generation before us that theologians declared Jesus was an Aryan. The damage we have done cannot simply be made good by the fact that Oberammergau shows on the stage of the Passion Play a "Jewish" Jesus who is often addressed as "Rabbi" and speaks a few more words of Hebrew.

To take Jesus seriously as a Jew means taking Judaism seriously and not only to long for the unity of the *one* people of God or to talk about it in conversation, but also to aim to win it back with all one's strength – the strength given by returning to God's will.

To replace "Christ" by "Jeschua" in the text of the play, as some people wanted, would not have made it clear that Jesus was a Jew and not a Christian. Jesus as a Jew implies the absolute validity of the Sermon on the Mount as the basis of the final way of life of God's people in readily identifiable communities of followers forming an interdependent, international network of the *shalom* throughout the world.

We Christians have ceased to regard the division between the church and synagogue as the worst scandal in the history of the world. Since we began to persecute the Jews we have avoided their question of whether the Messiah really came, as we attest. We have departed further and further from our origins and we have put over our own eyes the blindfold which we ascribed to the synagogue. The continuing divisions among God's people, together with Islam, which is the product of an earlier split, have torn our world apart. The blood from the body of the Messiah which we spilt when we fought each other, burned heretics and gassed Jews not only cries to heaven, it has also "fallen on us and our children".

Who accepts responsibility today?
The Gospels leave no doubt that Jesus, the Jew, died for his people, the Jewish people. He is the surety for God's loyalty to his people. In the 1990 Passion Play the chorus sings for the first time, "Oh Israel! Oh people of God! The blood of the lamb cleanses you from all guilt."
In his diary entry for Easter Sunday 1960 Dag Hammerskjöld, the UN Secretary General who died in the Congo while mediating in the civil war, expressed perfectly what Christian theology says about the death of Jesus: "forgiveness breaks the chain of causes because the person who forgives out of love takes responsibility for the consequences of what you did". Jesus broke the chain of causes of evil and indeed the consequences of the guilt for his death also, for which he died innocently, "for our sins". Jesus accepted full responsibility for the consequences of the words and deeds of those who called for the responsibility for his death to fall on them and their children.
We Christians have hardly followed him in this. In anti-Judaism we have repudiated him and, finally, in the holocaust we have burdened ourselves with a guilt which is hardly less than the guilt of those whose acts were accompanied by the acceptance of responsibility for themselves and their children. Jesus himself said they did not know what they were doing. Can this be said by any of us? Which of us accepts responsibility today?

No mercy for later generations
The words concerning responsibility for Christ's death are harsh in making it clear that there is no mercy for later generations. On the

contrary, it is they who are particularly affected by the consequences of the guilt for Christ's death. We, today, are affected by the consequences of the holocaust and the decisions which were prepared over centuries and which permitted it and brought it about. Although Passion Plays did not encourage the holocaust, they did not prevent it either. And today they should not serve to cover up our guilt now that we are beginning to realise the extent of the evil that was done.

Those watching the Passion Play in Oberammergau should, as the chorus repeatedly suggests, accept the idea that the story of Jesus' suffering tells us about our own cowardice and wickedness, our lack of faith, envy and resentment.

The spectator should regard himself as one of those who spoke the words about his own blood guilt and that of his children. Only in this way will he be able to meet the historical situation in which we all find ourselves today.

Munich, 2 February 1990   RUDOLF PESCH

Prof. Dr. Dr. Rudolf Pesch, a New Testament scholar, was proposed by the German Conference of Bishops as adviser to the Textual Commission of Oberammergau.

The Cast of the 1990 Passion Play

Christ
: Norz Martin
Reindl Stephan

Mary
: Burkhart Ursula
Petre Elisabeth

Prologue
: Huber Otto
Lück Carsten

Christ's apostles and followers

Peter
: Härtle Werner
Zwink Vitus

John
: Adam Michael
Heiland Robert

Judas
: Jablonka Max
Stückl Peter

Thomas — Mayr Johannes
Philip — Mayr Christian
Thaddeus — Steinecke Helmut
James the Elder — Albl Joseph
James the Younger — Dörfler Stephan
Simon — Reiser Korbinian
Andrew — Fellner Georg
Matthew — Lehneis Hans
Bartholomew — Lang Florian

Magdalene
: Schauer Andrea
Stuckenberger Helga

Simon of Bethany
: Eitzenberger Karl jun.
Gstaiger Guido

Lazarus	Zwink Dominikus
Martha	Wagner Gabriele
Mary Salome	Bierling Barbara
Mary the wife of Cleopas	Stückl Barbara
Angel	Hageneier Stephan

High Council (priests and scribes)

Caiaphas	Fischer Walter
	Wagner Martin
Annas	Führler Karl
	Stückl Benedikt
Nathaniel	Burkhart Anton jun.
	Müller Matthias
Archelaus	Fischer Leonhard jun.
	Preisinger Anton Klaus
Ezekiel	Bierling Kuno
	Eich Willi
Joseph of Arimathea	Reiser Richard
	Zwink Anton
Nicodemus	Feldmeier Hans jun.
	Lang Walter
Dathan	Härtle Karl
	Rutz Walter
Zadok	Pongratz Anton
Joshua	Lehneis Siegfried
Amiel	Magold Martin sen.
Rabinth	Bauer Siegfried
Dariabas	Allinger Karl sen.
Saras	Rutz Hugo
Amron	Schilcher Max
Samuel	Bierling Ernst sen.

Oziel	Dr. Kreuter Franz
Josaphat	Heimbach Anton
Nathan	Raab Karl
Aman	Zwink Werner
Aser	Breitsamter Melchior sen.
Gamaliel	Hochenleitner Ulrich
Gerson	Uhl Eduard
Jacob	Zwink Heinrich

Annas' servants

Esdras	Steidle Robert
Sidrach	Petter-Schwaiger Günther
Misael	Freisl Anton
Zotobabel (temple attendant)	Mang Otto

Herod and his servants

Herod	Maderspacher Anton
	Zwink Franz
Naasson	Bierprigl Helmut
Manasse	Kronthaler Valentin

Romans

Pilate	Burkhart Stephan
	Dr. Fischer Helmut
Longinus, captain	Fend Klement
	Rott Robert

Roman soldiers and executioners (speaking parts)

Lictor	Lischka Gerhard
Caspius	Maderspacher Ernst
Sabinus	Bierling Christian

Domitius	Pongratz Max jun.
Titus	Fussy Raimund
Milo	Bauer Alfred
Catilina	Richter Alfred
Faustus	Reiser Lothar
Nero	Eich Peter
Agrippa	Schuster Arnulf

Pilate's servants and advisers

Quintus	Bierling Ernst jun.
Aurelius	Schmid Michael
Claudius	Müller Werner
Pomponius	Pongratz Peter
Mela	Führler Hans
Silvus	Götz Karl-Heinz
Flavius	Schauer Georg

Traders in the Temple

Kosam	Feldmeier Hans sen.
Booz	Eich Gustav
Albion	Schmid Hans
Esron	Reiser Werner

Witnesses

Nun	Zigon Rolf
Eliab	Bierling Hans-Dieter
Gad	Schweiger Karl-Heinz
Eliezer	Utschneider Martin

Temple guards (speaking parts)

Selpha, captain	Lang Edmund
Malchus	Heigl Max jun.

Balbus	Müller Friedl
Panther	Eich Horst
Melchi	Schweiger Luitpold
Levi	Köpf Paul
Arphaxad	Schmid Hubert
Abdias	Steidle Stephan
Dan	Daubner Joseph jun.

Maidservants in Caiaphas' house

Agar	Wankmüller Michaela
Sara	Müller Kathrin

Men and women on the Way of the Cross

Simon the Cyrenian	Pongratz Anton
Veronica	Baumann Franziska
	Müller Christine
Weeping women	Klement Petra
	Niggl Andrea
	Pongratz Monika
	Straka Verena
	Streibl Stephanie
	Utschneider Brigitte

Thieves

Dismas	Lederer Jochen
Gesmas	Steidle Thomas
Barabbas	Schneller Theo

Temple guards, Roman soldiers, men, women and children of Jerusalem.

Music:

Conductors	Zwink Markus
	Hoffmann Ernst
	Troll Tosso
Soloists	
Soprano	Fischer Irmgard
	Strauss Maria
	Weinfurtner-Zwink Gabriele
Contralto	Fischer Caroline
	Pensberger Gertrud
	Schauer Antonie
Tenor	Eitzenberger Andreas
	Heiss Kurt
	Köpf Joseph
Bass	Breitsamter Gregor
	Buchwieser Heino
	Kotschenreuther Georg
Training of soloists	Gross Arthur

Chorus and Orchestra

Stage:

Stage manager (equipment and lightning)	Maurer Anton
Stage manager (scenery)	Müller Alfred
Workshop managers	Feldmeier Hans jun.
	Mangold Martin
Costumes manager	Jäger Ingrid

Weapons and armour	Breidenbach Martin
Prompters	Baab Erich
	Daisenberger Karl

Passion Play Committee, workshop craftsmen, organisation team of the Village of Oberammergau, stagehands, cloakroom attendants, ushers, members of the Fire Brigade and Red Cross.

Voice and speech training	Langer Brigitte
Deputy director (dramaturgy)	Huber Otto
Design	Georg Johann Lang (1889–1968; director of the Passion Play from 1922 to 1960)
Director	Stückl Christian

PROGRAMME

for the Oberammergau Passion Play 1990

Dress rehearsal	Thursday	17 May
General rehearsal	Saturday	19 May
Press performance	Sunday	20 May

Plays with Accomodations

MAY		JUNE		JULY		AUGUST		SEPTEMBER	
Monday	21	Friday	1	Sunday	1	Wednesday	1	Sunday	2
Wednesday	23	Sunday	3	Monday	2	Friday	3	Monday	3
Friday	25	Monday	4	Wednesday	4	Sunday	5	Wednesday	5
Sunday	27	Wednesday	6	Friday	6	Monday	6	Friday	7
Monday	28	Friday	8	Sunday	8	Wednesday	8	Sunday	9
Wednesday	30	Sunday	10	Monday	9	Friday	10	Monday	10
		Monday	11	Wednesday	11	Sunday	12	Wednesday	12
		Wednesday	13	Friday	13	Monday	13	Friday	14
		Friday	15	Sunday	15	Wednesday	15	Sunday	16
		Sunday	17	Monday	16	Friday	17	Monday	17
		Monday	18	Wednesday	18	Sunday	19	Wednesday	19
		Wednesday	20	Friday	20	Monday	20	Friday	21
		Friday	22	Sunday	22	Wednesday	22	Sunday	23
		Sunday	24	Monday	23	Friday	24	Monday	24
		Monday	25	Wednesday	25	Sunday	26	Wednesday	26
		Wednesday	27	Friday	27	Monday	27	Friday	28
		Friday	29	Sunday	29	Wednesday	29		
				Monday	30	Friday	31		

Plays without Accomodations

Saturday	26	Saturday	2	Saturday	7	Saturday	4	Saturday	1
		Saturday	9	Saturday	14	Saturday	11	Saturday	8
		Saturday	16	Saturday	21	Saturday	18	Saturday	15
		Saturday	23	Saturday	28	Saturday	25	Saturday	22
		Saturday	30					Saturday	29
								Sunday	30

3 rehearsals
20 repeat performances
75 main performances

98 performances

PUBLICATIONS
of the Oberammergau Passion Play

Illustrated Souvenir Book
"The Oberammergau Passion Play 1990"
in German and English
DM 19.80

Official Guide to the Oberammergau Passion Play
What you should know about Oberammergau
and the Passion Play
Published in German, Englisch and French
All languages DM 4.80

Slides
Individual series (6 slides)   DM 8.00
Gift pack (36 slides)   DM 48.00

Dedler Commemorative Brochure
The Life and Works of Rochus Dedler,
composer of the Passionsmusik
(German only)
DM 4.80

Text of the 1990 Passion Play
German, English and French
DM 6.00 all languages

© Published by the Village of Oberammergau